FRED ASTAIRE

FRED ASTAIRE

Michael Freedland

Grosset & Dunlap
A Filmways Company
Publishers • New York

Copyright © 1976 by Michael Freedland

All rights reserved
Published simultaneously in Canada
Library of Congress catalog card number: 77-80371
ISBN 0-448-14079-9 (hardbound)
ISBN 0-448-14080-2 (paperback)
Originally published in Great Britain
by W. H. Allen & Co. Ltd., London
First Grosset & Dunlap edition 1977
Printed in the United States of America

CONTENTS

FRED
ASTAIRE

There were still nearly thirty years to go when an American national magazine decided to tot up the credit and loss account of the twentieth century. When they came to choosing their 'Entertainer of the Century', they picked Fred Astaire.

If they had selected anyone else, the letters would have poured in and the complaints would have multiplied. How can you choose anything of the century with a quarter of it still to go? How can the Man of the Year be selected in September or the movie of the year be chosen in February? Yet such things do constantly happen and every time they do someone scoffs.

But no one did complain about the choice of Astaire. His was genuinely a household name, as vivid to the older generation as the memory of the Charleston and a stolen kiss in the jump seat of an open car. More important, their grandchildren knew it, too – some of them as well as that of the latest pop group who would consider themselves lucky to survive the season.

What was Fred Astaire's secret? Partly that he could put into a pair of feet the energy required to fly a jet plane yet make it all look like a glider swimming in a cool breeze. Partly because he could sing songs in a voice that of itself would never win any vocal prizes, but in a way that would make him the idol of the songwriters. Cole Porter, George Gershwin, Jerome Kern and Irving Berlin all said they would rather have him sing their songs than anyone else – because he not only had a sense of rhythm as instinctive as the desire to breathe but because he had a deep respect for the meaning of lyrics.

It was Kern who said of him: 'Astaire can't do anything bad.' And possibly the reason was the work he put into achieving that seemingly effortless pose. When he danced down a street, it was the result of weeks of planning every foot motion, almost every flex of his muscles – but it wouldn't have worked had he not made it seem as though he were doing it all on the spur of the moment, as naturally and easily as a small boy would kick a ball. It produced an incredible limiting factor to the vocabulary of the people who knew him. Invariably they would all choose the same word to describe him: perfectionist. Astaire's legacy has been to make the tap dance respectable.

Before Astaire there was ballet and 'the other sort', which usually amounted to the kind of thing chorus girls did. In vaudeville, there was the old soft shoe routine. From New Orleans, through the blackface minstrel shows and on to Broadway, performers like Zip Coon and Jim Crow – who themselves had something of an effect on the English language – added the 'buck and wing'. But it took Astaire to refine that quaint jazz shuffle into tap dancing and in turn to be regarded himself as a latter day Nijinsky.

To an actress, the chance to dance with Astaire was both the culmination of a dream and a demand for a work schedule so tough that it could bring her to tears. Yet in most cases he was that rare breed: a generous showman. Ann Miller said of him, 'It's as though I've always danced

3

with him. He has that way with women. He tried to do the steps that made her look good. I appreciate that. It's very unusual in a man dancer.'

There's probably only one person who will not accept that there was anything at all unusual about Astaire and that's himself.

He once said: 'I'm not one of those people who can say, "I was born in the world without a shirt to my back and when I was old enough to pour my own cup of coffee . . ." I can't go into that whole deal.'

In fact, he steadfastly refuses to live in the past or even reflect on what the rest of us would like to call his glories. Ask him why, and he'll reply that it simply isn't his 'racket'. The most important thing is that he's glad he 'made a buck'. He wouldn't add that he's also glad that he made a lot of oth_ people happy. But he did.

4

5

SHALL WE DANCE ?

Fred Astaire, at the age of 5.
Even then, he was dancing.

It was a combination of the discipline in the Austro-Hungarian Army and Prohibition in Nebraska that produced the Entertainer of the Century. If it hadn't have been for the first of those two factors, Fred Astaire would never have been born; had it not been for the second, he quite possibly might never have been a great star.

His father, Frederic Austerlitz, was one of three brothers, all of them officers serving Franz Josef in the Austro-Hungarian Army; Frederic, a mere subaltern, Otto and Ernest rather more senior. They came from a family of brewers, but had decided to make the Army their career instead. Their mother's maiden name was Astaire.

Frederic was a handsome chap with a curly moustache. Out of uniform he wore a homburg with a crease in the front which made it resemble a Boy Scout's hat. But somehow, when that was combined with a bow tie and a tweed coat, it gave him the look of a suave opera singer.

His brother Ernest had a similar moustache – in fact it was much the same as Kaiser Wilhelm affected – and was tall and slim. He was also very conscious of his importance as an officer in the Imperial Army, for when he saw Frederic approach him and then fail to salute, he had his younger brother arrested and incarcerated in the divisional guard-house. It was the final straw for Frederic, he decided he had had enough, and as quickly as he could decently manage it, he left the Army, his homeland and family and set sail for America.

He settled in Omaha, Nebraska, got a job in a leather firm and there he met and fell in love with a local beauty named Ann Geilus. She was a schoolteacher and still a teenager when she married Frederic, who was about ten years older. The year of the wedding was 1896. A year later, Mrs Austerlitz gave birth to a baby girl. They called her Adele. Eighteen months afterwards, the family increased still further. Their second child was a boy. They named him Frederick – the final 'k' to the name making it look more American than the way the child's father spelt his.

He immediately became known simply as Fred, or Freddie, the day he was born, 10 May 1899. Adele, meanwhile had become 'Delly'.

At the age when most other children are considered due for nursery education, Adele was enrolled at Chambers' Dancing Academy and was soon regarded as the star attraction when the school put on its shows. Contrary to legend, Fred merely went along there for a ride in the family horse and buggy, when his mother took Adele to her lessons, and then collected her.

Freddie's involvement was soon to become more definite; he was no more than four years old when a big adventure beckoned. He heard he was going for a two-day train ride – to New York.

They had come without any introduction to the city other than their father's theatrical newspaper, although this was to prove useful. From it, they cut out an advertisement for a dancing school run by a Mr Claude Alvienne.

Fred was conscious of the opportunity he now had. 'Mr Alvienne is going to make me a star,' he told Adele, who replied 'Don't be silly!' Well, Fred was learning to dance. He was also beginning to sing – in fact, he was singing more than he was dancing at this stage, and he wasn't yet five years old.

It was while at Mr Alvienne's establishment that Fred decided on the sort of dancer he was going to be – or rather Mr Alvienne decided for him. At the back of the school's stage, he set up two wedding cakes, each with a collection of electric light bulbs glowing from it, and in front of them a bride and bridegroom. Adele, all in white, was the bride, Fred was the bridegroom. He wore tails, white tie – and a top hat. In the annals of the theatre, an historic moment, that. The fact that his ensemble was complemented by a pair of black silk knickerbockers should not be allowed to diminish the importance of that moment.

The two danced on the cakes and on the stage around them. Mr and Mrs Alvienne told them how good they were.

It was at Keyport, New Jersey, that an even more historic moment dawned. In the small theatre at the end of the pier, with the waves of the Atlantic Ocean lapping the supports below, Adele and Fred Austerlitz did their wedding cake dance and people paid to see them do it. Or at least they paid to see Adele and Fred Astaire. At five years old, the Austerlitz children had changed their names. Austerlitz, their mother was advised, wouldn't look good on theatre bills; so she searched for alternatives and decided on her mother-in-law's maiden name. It not only looked better, it looked French. Their professional debut had to come in style. And they got fifty dollars for their efforts – the very first money Fred and Adele earned.

In December 1905, a critic wrote: 'Two little ones, Adele and Fred, give an electrical dancing novelty in vaudeville.' It was one of the first of thousands of such reviews.

It was also one of a crop of reviews that took these impressive youngsters to what was known in the vaudeville business as the Big Time. Whenever he had the opportunity, Frederic Austerlitz Senior, used to leave Omaha and drop into New York as much to see the Broadway shows and get to know the important show people as to visit his family. An attractive character, Mr Austerlitz had the gift of being able to make friends easily. One of these friends was Frank Vincent, who booked acts for the famed Orpheum Circuit – one of the huge chains of theatres that managed to slice the world of American vaudeville between them. The man from the circuit saw the Astaires and said he liked what he saw.

The Astaires had two things in their favour that other child entertainers did not always have – for most of them appeared to have run away from home – a mother to watch every move they made and even more important to give them private tuition in more than just the art of tapping their toes. As they went from place to place on trains, to hotel rooms and backstage in the theatres, their mother took her bundle

Under the guidance of their mother, Ann Geilus Astaire, Fred and Adele toured the vaudeville circuit, doing two shows a day all across America.

of school books and gave them lessons. Meanwhile, she changed her name, too – to Astaire.

Soon, however, theatre managers stopped asking for them. Mr. Austerlitz and his wife were intelligent parents and decided not to fight what appeared to be the writing on the wall. They agreed that their children would leave the stage and go to school.

They had also found a new home. It was at Highwood Park; the residential part of Weekhawken in New Jersey. To the children's parents, one of the most important features of this new environment was that it offered a good state school. So for the first time, Adele and Fred sat in a classroom and at the same sort of desks as any other children of their age; and Mrs Astaire's training was paying off. The

lessons she had given Fred meant that he was able to compete on more than merely equal terms with boys and girls of his age. Within days he went up a class so that he was with children a year older than he was.

Fred himself says he hates looking back on those days. 'It's boring for an old-timer,' he insists. But, as long as they have been able to find an audience, the people who remembered the Astaires have been talking about the kids they knew at school. They recalled that Fred used to hate being asked to give an impromptu performance, either at school or at some social function. He'd shrug his shoulders or mop his curly brown hair, but he wouldn't dance. If they insisted that he do something for them, he would compromise with a rendition of 'Asleep In The Deep', which his mother had taught him.

For two years the Astaires were like two ordinary children at an ordinary school. And then their mother decided they should try to think about the theatre again. With her they went to see the latest shows, all the big acts at both the neighbourhood and the New York theatres. Among the acts they saw again and again were a husband and wife team of ballroom dancers who for a time dominated the exhibition dancing scene, Vernon and Irene Castle.

Mrs Astaire also changed their school, and while continuing to coach them, enrolled the pair at Ned Wayburn's dancing school, which she rightly considered to be a training ground for stars. If all his pupils didn't end up with a Number One dressing room, it was unlikely to be Mr Wayburn's fault. As a director of shows, he was unsurpassed and Flo Ziegfeld bore testimony to that fact by frequently employing him. He did more than teach Adele and Fred new dance steps. He wrote them a vaudeville routine – and charged their mother $1,000 for it, which she paid in quarterly instalments.

The act Wayburn wrote put Fred in what he liked to consider his favorite stance, with a baseball bat in his hand and a ballplayer's outfit on his back. The act even had a name – 'A Rainy Saturday'.

They worked hard, Fred much harder than Adele, for he was beginning to take the job of being an entertainer seriously. He gave up playing in the streets and concentrated on working, meticulously pacing out the details of the toe dance and the soft shoe routine. Adele, meanwhile, thought it was a lot of fun and enjoyed playing the clown. Yet when she danced it was as natural and perfect as anything ever seen in a ballet.

But it was difficult to get anyone to appreciate just how perfect either she or her brother was. Not until Wayburn got them a booking at a benefit show at the Broadway Theatre did anyone see their act. And when they did, it all seemed well worth the effort. A critic reported they were a 'clever singing and dancing team' and as a result they were given their big chance at one of the smartest vaudeville theatres in New York, Proctor's on Fifth Avenue. Topping the bill was a Mr Douglas Fairbanks.

If they thought they had reached perfection, the result of the engage-

ment at Proctor's soon put their careers into perspective. Not only were they opening the show – a killing spot in those days when vaudeville was as much a part of everyday life as a television screen is today – but they were not very good.

They returned to the theatre that night despondent. When they saw the running order of acts for the evening performance, they were even more distraught. Their name wasn't among them. When they asked why, the answer was all too clear – they had been fired.

Show business has a phrase for what the Astaires were doing now. They were 'picking up time' – whatever work they could get, sandwiched in between the daily lessons their mother still gave them. Not only were they picking up time, but they were picking up small time, the sort of vaudeville that never saw a real headliner. It seemed that the Big Time was slipping firmly away from their grasp and for seasoned vaudeville entertainers like themselves that was a sad situation.

Things seemed to get better when they were earning $150 a week and had the second from last position on the bill. But more than once they were second to a dog act and the dogs had the best dressing room. Another time, they had to climb a ladder to get to their own dressing room because a troupe of trained seals had to have the only one downstairs.

Even though the kids and their mother were frequently in one part of the US, or maybe in Canada, while their father was in another, they were a close family. Mr Austerlitz would come to visit the travelling players whenever he could, and would help supplement their income. When they failed to pick up enough time, they had to live on almost non-existent savings. When they were working, their salary cheque had to cover the cost of those train trips from one tank town – the showbiz term that summed up all the love and frustration of vaudeville circuitry – to another, as well as their costumes and the money they had to pay to the keepers of theatrical lodging houses.

Sometimes, things were so desperate that Mrs Astaire had to pawn a small diamond to see them through the week. On another celebrated occasion, she cut an egg in half and divided it among the children.

Matters were complicated still further by that problem of Prohibition in the State of Nebraska. In 1916, the state went dry and Mr Austerlitz had to start thinking about getting a new job. That was a lot more easily said than done, but he changed his name to Astaire, and kept trying. If his children had ever contemplated a premature retirement, this new turn of events had to put the idea completely out of their minds. So they stayed in small-time vaudeville and continued to make tours of the theatres.

They went back to work at the end of each summer – or, rather, they chased the work where it lay. They would play anywhere that there was a vaudeville theatre ready to have them. If the theatre manager didn't like an act, he would write a report to the circuit head office. If the report was really bad, there was a fair chance the act would lose its next booking.

Life was never at a lower ebb for the two Astaires than when the pair hit Detroit. Fred was no more than fifteen, but he and Adele were old enough to be right in the middle of a vaudeville artists' strike. They were not members of the 'union', the White Rats, but just the same they were laid off and were short of money, too.

When they did get the odd spot on a vaudeville bill, they were still being talked of as a pair of kids, Adele and her little brother. But things were changing and when finally, they got back on to the Orpheum Circuit, between them the Astaires were now earning the fabulous sum of $225 a week. What was more, they were working with big stars now. One of these was a couple called Eduardo and Elisa Cansino. Like the Astaires they, too, were brother and sister, but unlike them at the time, they topped every bill they were on. They were the leading team of Spanish dancers in the business and both Fred and Adele were captivated by their poise and style. Adele, in fact, confesses to this day that she fell madly in love with Eduardo. A generation later, Fred was still influenced by the pair. As a result of that influence, he helped give the first big chance to Eduardo's daughter. By then she was known as Rita Hayworth.

The Orpheum office obviously thought they were getting it right often enough to offer them as much as $350 for a single week's work, which was incredible money for a pair of teenagers in those days Their first dance routine with Fred as a detective arresting Adele, a gangster's moll, brought the house down at the Palace Theatre in Chicago and brought them a string of further bookings, too.

Reviewers were noticing the Astaires, too. Most of them deciding without a shadow of doubt that the real star in the family was Adele. The Philadelphia *North American* declared: 'The bill began with a pair of excellent dancers, Fred and Adele Astaire. The girl who was also the possesser of remarkably good looks, being especially graceful of movement.'

They not only sought out and obtained new bookings but new material, too. They would go round the music publishers' offices, pop into the booths where the pluggers were demonstrating songs and would then dance to the melodies banged out by the pianists. At Remicks, in New York, a young plugger was so impressed by the way they performed that he said he would like nothing more than to write a brand new show for this unusual pair of kid dancers. They told him they would like nothing better themselves and made a note of his name – George Gershwin.

The Astaires were back in New York on Fred's seventeenth birthday. A scout from the Shubert Brothers, the toughest, most ruthless impresarios of the age, set out to see them. The scout went backstage, knocked on their dressing room doors and invited the pair to take part in the next Shubert show. They accepted. Had they turned down the offer, they would have been turning down Broadway.

By 1920, Fred and Adele had begun to make a name for themselves as the brightest young dance team in vaudeville.

FOR GOODNESS SAKE

In a typical pose.

Broadway in 1917 was more than just a place name. It had already become a word in the English language, even if you couldn't find it in a dictionary. But you didn't have to look it up; to anyone who had ever spent a couple of cents for a seat in the gallery it meant Big Time show business – and the capital letters were part of the definition. When America entered World War One, Broadway had also somehow come to symbolise patriotism.

There were parades through the street; flags in almost every show. Those productions that were not so blatantly banner-waving were helping the cause Woodrow Wilson had ordained for America – simply by being escapist. And *Over The Top* was that kind of show, its billing was littered with names that are now part of Broadway and Tin Pan Alley folklore. The score was by Sigmund Romberg, Harold Atteridge wrote some of the sketches and Justine Johnstone and Mary Eaton were the leads. It also featured Fred and Adele Astaire. Before long, they were joined by Ed Wynn, a tall slightly overweight comedian who wore spectacles without lenses in them. Fred and the older Wynn became firm friends and cemented their friendship on the golf course.

But the friendship of Wynn and Astaire was stronger than the show. It had started off at New Haven, Connecticut by being called the *Nine O'Clock Revue* and was very popular with the students at Yale. Possibly this approval from an institution of learning was the reason the artists were quaintly introduced with this note in the show programme: 'To make the lucidity of the libretto conspicuous, the following musical interruptions take place . . .' The show lasted a mere seventy-eight performances, but these were enough for the Astaires to be noticed.

The Shubert Brothers – Lee and Jake, who six years earlier had made the biggest Broadway discovery of all time, Al Jolson – were among those who did notice. They signed the Astaires for *The Passing Show of 1918*, the next production at the 'flagship' of their empire, the Winter Garden. It was probably Broadway's most attractive theatre and the one which Jolson had been making his own.

In *The Passing Show*, both Fred and Adele were adorned with chicken feathers for a number called 'Twit, Twit, Twit, Twit' and Adele sang 'I Can't Make My Feet Behave' – although, in fact, she made them behave exceedingly well. They were billed as 'Fred and Adele Astaire, New Songs and Smart Dances'.

The Passing Show was followed by a production with music by Fritz Kreisler called *Apple Blossoms* – the most notable feature of which was not the world-famous violinist's score, but the fact that it was produced by Charles Dillingham, a rival of the Shubert Brothers and also one of the main competitors to Florenz Ziegfeld.

The day the Astaires met him for the first time, Dillingham was sitting in his office quite obviously overcome from the effects of a long hot New York summer. He was mopping his balding head with a piece of blotting paper. 'Well, kids, what do you expect to get?' he asked. Fred, up till then thought of as too shy to ask the directions to the theatre, replied: 'Five hundred and fifty dollars!'

While the show was having a trial run at Atlantic City, Dillingham took the Astaires out to dinner at the resort's best hotel. Then, after the opening in New York, he wined and dined them in the manner to which he, as a scion of one of the city's Society families, had become accustomed. In some ways, this was also the introduction of the Astaires into society. Fred had few friends, though, and was content to save his contacts with other people for when he was on stage.

In *Apple Blossoms*, the contact came from the almost thunderous applause of the audience – an audience who had been informed of the Astaire's presence at the Globe Theatre on Broadway and 46th Street through a programme which listed the cast in their section of the show like this:

> *Julie*   Miss Lena Parker
> *Polly*   Miss Juanita Fletcher
> *Molly*   Adele Astaire
> *Johnny*   F. Astaire

The friendship between Gershwin and the Astaires was blooming like the *Apple Blossoms* of the title. Together, they would go to night clubs and spot the talent whom each would predict would one day 'make it'. They would play 'in' games on the piano together, with Fred playing a chord that struck Gershwin as fascinating; 'What was that?' he would ask. 'What was that?' Occasionally, the roles would change, with George demonstrating a dance or two that Fred had to promise to think about.

Looking back now it is certain that the Astaires contributed more to *Apple Blossoms* than anyone else. It is also certain that without them, it would never have run as long as it did; the Broadway histories now record that the show ran for a total of 256 performances. When Charles Dillingham looked for a follow up, he believed he had found it with *The Love Letter*. It opened in October 1921 at the same theatre as *Apple Blossoms* and again with John Charles Thomas in the lead. The credits also included William Le Baron writing the book and lyrics (as he had done for *Apple Blossoms*) and Victor Jacobi, who had shared the music score of the previous show with Kreisler, and was now providing all the music himself. The show also had the Astaires.

The Love Letter was no great masterpiece, in fact, there appeared to be no love lost at all between the show and the patrons. After thirty-one wilting performances, it died.

The show did not close, however, before it could be seen by a man selling ties in a Fifth Avenue store. Fred was buying a tie and the man selling it to him was called Alex Aarons. His father owned the shop as well as being a top man in one of the biggest American theatrical production firms. Aarons junior, had no desire to sell ties indefinitely. In fact, the sooner he could get out from behind the counter and go into show business himself, the better he'd like it. He'd like it even more, he said, if the Astaires would join him. This was not an invitation that could be turned down lightly, providing that Charles Dillingham

After successful runs on Broadway and in London with Stop Flirting *(called* For Goodness Sake *in New York), the Astaires opened in a show written by George and Ira Gershwin called* Black Eyed Susan. *The name was soon changed to* Lady Be Good.

would 'lend' them for the run of the show. With Aarons' father's connections, it seemed as if it couldn't go wrong. He also had another ace up his sleeve. Almost by the way, he added that there was a young man ready to do the score. His name, George Gershwin.

With the memory of George's wish that day in the Remick's song plugger's booth still quite fresh, it represented the clinch to a deal being carried off. Fred and Adele talked it over with their agent and they agreed it was a show they wanted to do just as soon as *The Love Letter* closed. And Dillingham raised no objection either. The only problem was that Gershwin was not available to do the entire score. The young man had just had a fantastic success with his hit 'Swanee' which was to prove, in fact, the most profitable number in his entire career – and was contracted to the showman George White to provide the music for his latest 'Scandals' production. But he did promise to produce a few numbers for the Aarons' show, which was going to be called *For Goodness Sake*.

They were number six in the list of artists appearing, but signing the contract for the show was the most sensible thing they had yet done in their careers. Robert Benchley, writing in the New York magazine *Life*, summed up the reaction of most people who saw it:

'There isn't much to say about *For Goodness Sake* that you couldn't say about most musicals except that the Astaires are in it. When they dance, everything seems brighter and their comedy alone would be good enough to carry them through, even if they were to stop dancing (which God forbid).'

An extraordinary amount of hard work had got the Astaires to the point where Charles Dillingham decided to keep them for himself. He wasn't going to be persuaded by Aarons or anyone else to release them from his contract this time, and he was about to pay them for the privilege – to the tune of $1,000 a week.

Now, he was going to build a show entirely around the brother and sister who, to use the Broadway cliché, had taken the town by storm. He was doing so at a time when people wanted to know all they could about Adele and Fred.

Dillingham's new show was called *The Bunch and Judy*. Most of the critics liked it, although one writer described the performance as 'an artless piece', which didn't seem to bode well for the stars. But the audience loved the run-around – this time to a piece called 'How Do You Do, Katinka?', and Heywood Broun wrote in the *New York World*, 'Fred and Adele are the most gracious young dancers available in the world of musical comedy. Indeed, the Astaires are distinctly attractive even when they are not in motion, and once they begin to dance they are among the immortals.'

But if the critics were basically sympathetic, the audiences were plainly much less warm about the show than they had been for the previous Astaire appearances. It showed, too, in the box office takings.

After just over three weeks, *The Bunch and Judy* closed, and from that moment on, the Astaires called it 'The Bust and Judy'. It was the first time they had starred in their own show and it was the biggest flop they had experienced since their names were removed from the bill at Proctor's Fifth Avenue. As far as they were concerned, they weren't really the stars they had genuinely believed themselves to be. And they wondered if Dillingham thought they were, either. He decided not to take up the option he had on them for $1,250 a week and didn't even give them a Christmas present. Alex Aarons, however, backed his hunch. If *The Bunch and Judy* failed, it was because it wasn't much of a show, not that the Astaires weren't good performers. He wanted to extend his operations and he thought that Fred and Adele deserved to have a wider audience than they had experienced so far – even with a whole string of country-wide vaudeville tours behind them.

He had been having talks in London with Sir Alfred Butt, an MP, who was also a theatre producer. The Astaires, he told Butt, were made to measure for London and he had just the vehicle for them. As for the dancers, he simply asked: 'How would you like to do *For Goodness Sake* in London?'

It didn't take much to convince Adele and Fred that this was an opportunity they just could not afford to miss. They were going to London and were going there as stars. For the crossing they were sailing on the *Aquitania* – first class, of course. When they arrived in London, they would be accommodated at the Savoy, which really was the pinnacle of success.

When they got to London, they were shown the sights, smelled the sooty London air and announced they loved every inch of the place. They wondered about the theatres, though. The stages looked different and sitting in the stalls for the first night of a revue that floundered before their eyes was an experience that sent shivers up and down their spines.

There were changes in the routines, changes in the dialogue and changes in the other players. One of the New York numbers 'Tra La La' was withdrawn and in its place was a new Gershwin song, 'Stairway to Paradise', which before long was to rank as one of the composer's greatest standards. But the biggest change of all – apart from the rise in status of the Astaires – was the title. *For Goodness Sake* became, without any reasonable explanation, *Stop Flirting*.

The show opened at the Royal Court Theatre, Liverpool, early in 1923. With what the young Astaires must have thought was fairly typical British phlegm, the *Liverpool Dispatch* gave them a warm welcome to a city which would itself one day have an important place in the British pop scene. It said: 'The hit of the evening was a comedy dance by an exceedingly clever American couple, Miss Adele and Mr Fred Astaire, whose dancing throughout is a feature of the programme.'

It was the same story in Edinburgh and again when they finally opened in London. It was at the Shaftesbury Theatre on 20 May 1923, an evening represented in the Astaire memory by a sea of women in evening dresses and men in stiff white shirt fronts – all of them calling out 'core', 'core' after every twirl on stage. The gallery was ecstatic and, far away in a haze, there were the equally emotional shouts from

that unique institution of the British theatre, the 'pit'. Adele and 'her partner Fred' had all the encouragement they needed. At the end of the show, Adele went down to the footlights and told the still cheering audience: 'My brother and I thank you from the bottom of our hearts and – and we want you all to come and have tea with us tomorrow.' Fred was less forthcoming: 'She said it,' he added.

The *New York Times* thought the reaction important enough to print a telegram received from London. 'Adele and Fred Astaire by their dancing carried away the audience and the number of encores they received actually impeded the action of the piece.' The headline said it all, 'Or as one says in the cruder western hemisphere, they stopped the show.'

It was the beginning of a love affair with London. Fifty years later Fred was still saying: 'I may even live there one day.' As much as anything it was a love affair with a way of life. Britain had emerged from the war shaken, but determined to have a good time. The twenties were gay and exciting for people who had money and a desire to enjoy themselves and there was no Prohibition or its effects to make chasing that good time the sordid experience it was in the States. The white ties in the audience summed it all up – if a black bow was spotted the Astaires felt that the show was running down. But the big thing that happened during the run of *Stop Flirting* was a visit to the theatre by the Prince of Wales. The show had just moved from the Shaftesbury to the Queens and the Prince was sitting in the eighth row with a party of friends, a lady to his left. He obviously enjoyed the experience, for later in the week he came back again and this time went round to the Astaires' dressing rooms after the performance.

There were altogether ten visits by the Prince of Wales and other members of his family to *Stop Flirting*, during which time the heir to the British throne had become the idol of the kid from Omaha.

The Astaires had become part of London society themselves, and the centre of a host of advertising campaigns. They lent their names to toothbrushes and pick-me-ups and succeeded in convincing a somewhat gullible public that their lives would never be the same without these products.

If London was the scene of the Astaires' greatest triumphs to date, it was also the place where they first experienced a family bereavement. During the run of the show, their mother had gone home to the States. Her husband still was ill and not responding to medical treatment and she thought she ought to be near him. They were together when he died. Sir Alfred Butt gave Fred and Adele the news, but the legend was that the show must go on – and that night it did.

There had been six hundred performances of *Stop Flirting* and Fred and Adele didn't miss one of them. But in August 1924, they announced that they were packing up and going home. They weren't bored with the show, even less were they growing tired of London.

On April 14, 1926, Lady Be Good *opened in London. As always, Ann Astaire accompanied her children on tour.*

But the strain of dancing what they worked out to be a total of 10,000 miles in the one show was telling – particularly on Adele. She had been to see her doctor and he ordered her to stop immediately and take a complete rest.

On the final night at the Strand Theatre, the audience didn't know what to say either. But they reacted much more directly, they threw flowers on to the stage as well as anything else that was accessible and safe. It was the most incredible experience either of the Astaires had yet had on any stage. But there were to be more – and soon. For the moment, Adele admitted she was homesick. Fred said it was a matter of commitments in New York. Guy Bolton had written a new show and Alex Aarons was going to produce it again. They had to go now because the New Yorkers had such short memories and they were frightened they would be forgotten. 'But we can always come back,' said Fred. It was a promise to be kept.

Lady Be Good ran in New York for 330 performances and introduced such classic songs as "Fascinating Rhythm" and "The Man I Love."

They were all set for what even then looked like being their biggest opportunity so far. Fred and Adele were going to get $1,750 a week, with a promise of $250 more when they went on tour. Most important of all, they were finally going to do a complete show with George Gershwin.

The package handed to the Astaires by Aarons was for a production called *Black Eyed Susan*, a species that seemed constantly to crop up in song titles of the period but which they both agreed was a fairly uninspired name for a show. Yet it was going to be Broadway again and it would be the first opportunity since the disaster of *Bunch and Judy* to show New York what London had already discovered, that they now were really big stars.

It was an almost identically enticing prospect for George Gershwin. For the first time, he was contracted to do an entire score for a show, with his brother Ira writing the lyrics. George was still barely twenty-six-years-old, but he had already stormed his way to the top of the American musical scene, both with a rash of hit standards and his much more serious 'Rhapsody in Blue'. To date, there had been no formal partnership agreement with any lyricist although many of his early songs were with Irving Caesar and more recently with Buddy De Sylva. Just occasionally, he and Ira would work together as they had done in *For Goodness Sake* and in the show *Primrose*. But in this, his elder brother shared the lyric credits with a man called Desmond Carter and, as in his whole life, had been very much in George's shadow. In *For Goodness Sake* Ira didn't even have the self-confidence to write under his own name. Instead, he adopted the pseudonym of Arthur Francis.

The contract for *Black Eyed Susan* was signed the moment Fred and Adele had stepped down the gangplank of the *Homeric* in New York, and before they were finally cleared through customs. Fred rested the important document on one of his cabin trunks and scribbled his name at the foot of the page, before handing it over to Adele.

Black Eyed Susan didn't stay so named for very long. Before the Gershwins had completed the score, Aarons and Freedley had decided on a title they thought would be much more appealing. It would be called, they announced, *Lady Be Good*.

The *New York Times* spared no compliments to describe their dancing on the Liberty stage that night in December 1924, if it did get a little pen-tied:

> It is agile, clever, tricky, whatever you like to say about it. What really comes along is more elusive and vital than these. The art of words cannot say it. Just as Sullivan wrote the comedy of music, this art of the Astaires is the comedy of the dance. It alone can express itself.
>
> The show as such shows go is a good one. Above all there was the unique Astaire style. The dancing itself remains inexplicable. It is abstract as music is, scarcely imitative at all, quite free and completely itself.

Jock Whitney, the future publisher of the New York *Herald Tribune* and the man who would be the boss of the Technicolor empire as well as eventually Ambassador to the Court of St James's, was a close friend of both Fred and Adele. With them, he went to night clubs and to the race track.

The owners of the Trocadero wanted Fred and Adele to dance there each night, in competition to another club that was boasting its own team of ballroom dancers. The Astaires talked about it and said they could make enough money to buy themselves a Rolls Royce. They would do so only if they got five thousand dollars a week for it.

They got their five thousand, but voluntarily cut the figure to three thousand for the last two of the five weeks for which they were engaged. Business by then had begun to fall off and the rival club had already shut up shop. They had enough money to buy the car – but decided to wait for it. Soon, they would be in the most convenient place of all for buying a Rolls – London.

After 330 performances and a short tour, *Lady Be Good* was booked to open at London's Empire Theatre on 14 April 1926.

In between, they went to Paris for a short holiday, and had a try-out in Liverpool. When the curtains at the newly-redecorated Empire finally parted for the first performance of the show in London, the audience was ecstatic.

At first, everything about this London tour was centred on the show. Again, Fred would rehearse until well past midnight, and occasionally Adele was working out on the sloping stage with him. When opening night arrived, the dividends of the usual Astaire ration of hard work came in the response of the audience and – as always – of the critics.

The Times used the sort of language it normally reserved for what it liked to call 'events of historic moment'. Said its anonymous critic: 'Columbus may have danced with joy at discovering America, but how he would have cavorted had he also discovered Fred and Adele Astaire!'

The *New York Times* informed the folks back home:

Probably the warmest welcome ever given by London to an American actor or actress was that accorded tonight to Fred and Adele Astaire.... Enthusiasm mounted during the highly successful progress of *Lady Be Good*. It conceived such a liking for them that their first applause tonight was a signal for a loud and long demonstration. *Lady Be Good* seems to be in for a long run.

It was. Even more important, the Astaires were in for a long run at the top of the social ladder in British society – with their mother coming along not merely for the ride, but with her own unique brand of criticism if she felt they were falling behind their own harsh standards.

People were mostly interested in the friendship they were building up with the Royal Family. While Fred cemented his admiration and liking for the Prince of Wales and Prince George, Adele appeared to be getting on very well with the Duchess of York, now the Queen Mother. The Duchess invited her to tea one day at her Bruton Street house, in Mayfair, and suggested that perhaps she might like to come and see 'the baby'. The 'baby' is now Queen Elizabeth II.

Meanwhile, the Duke of York, who ten years later would become George VI, was sharing his brothers' fascination with Fred Astaire, the dancer and, reversing the situation, with Astaire the dresser. He thought it a marvellous idea that each pair of trousers hanging in Fred's wardrobe should have its own set of braces, instead of them having to be changed every time he put on a new pair of trousers. He was also fascinated as to why Fred kept his dancing shoes hanging upon the wall and not lying on the floor. It was, he explained, the best way to be sure that none of the mice which populated the Empire would nip the Astaire toes as he put on his shoes.

Princes, peers and mere socialites were making both Fred and Adele the toast of the town. At a London society ball, Gordon Selfridge the American millionaire boss of London's biggest department store, paid sixty pounds to dance with Adele. The profits of the ball went towards the Theatrical Ladies Guild and no one quibbled when Adele's services were auctioned and went up to the sixty pounds from a first bid of five.

'Mr Selfridge is really a good waltzer,' she declared. 'A rare thing nowadays.'

It was rare indeed. In fact, London was in the grip of Charleston fever and, Adele complained, was not doing it very well.

The Prince of Wales had now mastered the dance, too, and soon the Astaires would be responsible for teaching him a still newer step, the Black Bottom. It happened on the last night of *Lady Be Good*, the 326th performance of the show and the very last live production of any kind at the Empire Theatre.

Everyone knew that night in 1927 that the theatre was being pulled down and that this would be an important gala occasion. Celebrities from every branch of British life had bought tickets for the evening. The Danish ballerina, Adeline Genee whom Fred and Adele had seen so often as children, had taken a box for the evening. So had the Prince of Wales – although he hadn't taken the precaution to book in advance and only a personal call from the Prince to Astaire had done the trick. Fred had to ask the management to persuade another patron to give up his own seats.

As far as the Astaires – and the press – were concerned, it was fortunate that the deal for the box was made. The Prince and his party put a royal finish on an evening that has gone down in British theatrical history. The Empire, which started life as a Victorian music hall, shook with shrieks from the audience. The people in the stalls were as keen to see the Prince in full evening dress dancing at the back of his box as they were to watch Fred and Adele do the run-around on stage.

After the show, the Astaires and Jock Whitney followed the Royal group to a party at St James's Palace. There, Fred did a few steps himself, pulled Whitney on to the floor – and told him to demonstrate the latest dance craze. After his solo performance, the Prince asked Jock for a lesson. Whitney obliged and the Prince learned how to master the Black Bottom. As Adele recalled: 'And he had the bottom to do it, too. I'll tell you that!'

The biggest problem the Astaires had to face now was competition – the competition they alone presented to themselves. Every time they were pronounced sensational – and it seemed they constantly were – it meant only that the next time they were going to have to be even more exceptional.

It was in that situation that Fred and Adele Astaire embarked on a new show called *Smarty*.

They had had the usual rapturous response from British provincial audiences in the short tour that followed the closure of *Lady Be Good* in London, and with it of the Empire Theatre. On the voyage home on the *Homeric*, they had taken life nice, easy and satisfied. Keeping them company on board ship was their Rolls, and for them this was the symbol that counted. It represented all the glittering success they had had in their short lives – after all, they were both still in their twenties.

Home again in New York, Alex Aarons and Vinton Freedley discussed their plans for the next show. *Smarty* would have a score by the Gershwins and a book by Robert Benchley and also the usual pre-Broadway tour. When it was ready, there was a brand new theatre waiting for them, the Alvin, formed from the first syllables of the names of ALEx Aarons and VINton Freedley.

The trouble was that *Smarty* never looked ready. From the first dress rehearsal on the try-out tour, it seemed the Astaires were finally due to get the bird, and – to adopt the show-business parlance – that bird looked like being a turkey. Things appeared so bad at the Shubert Theatre in Philadelphia that Vinton Freedley called for a second dress rehearsal immediately after the first. When that ended about three hours before most people in the city were sitting down for breakfast, the co-producer announced the worst: The show only stood a chance if at least seventy-five per cent of it was thrown out of the window.

Benchley scribbled furiously and then gave up – because he couldn't find the time to continue the rewriting job. Finally, Fred Thompson and Paul Gerard Smith were brought in to start almost completely from scratch – while *Smarty* in its original form played to abysmal business, first in Philadelphia and then in Washington.

The show finally was considered to be as ready as it could be. On 22 November 1927, Fred put on his red and green bathrobe and, as never before, hoped it would prove as lucky as it had been that night in Connecticut five years before.

Perhaps the robe *was* lucky. Or perhaps it was simply that the combination of the Gershwin songs and the sheer tenacity and brilliance of the Astaires' dancing couldn't make the show anything but a hit. Perhaps, too, the change of title had something to do with it. *Smarty* had become *Funny Face*, yet another of those titles that have come to symbolise Fred and Adele Astaire.

Funny Face was a smash by anyone's definition. But on the night when everything went right, without a single untoward event, that was the moment Fred decided to remain behind at the theatre. With

No sooner did the Astaires return home than their producers had another show ready for them. This time it was Funny Face, *with book by Robert Benchley and music by the Gershwins.*

no one around, and with that sole rehearsal light on the stage, he would try out yet more new steps or seek to perfect a routine he alone thought was less than it should be.

Adele's birthday always became an occasion for celebration at the theatre where she and Fred were performing. While in *Funny Face* Fred had his 'gift' sent round to her dressing room. This time it wasn't from Cartiers. The note at one end of a silk ribbon read: 'To Adele, from a devoted admirer.' A lovely thought? Not exactly. At the other end of the ribbon was a Tibetan mountain goat which Fred had persuaded a keeper of the Central Park Zoo to let him borrow.

The doorman admitted he had some doubts about the enterprise, but Fred assured him that it would be all right. The goat stood there at the entrance to the flower-bedecked dressing room while Adele let out something closely resembling a shriek. Since, should the occasion arise, she was never one to baulk at using the sort of language that sailors find familiar, she possibly said something else, too.

The long and short of it was that she told the doorman to turn the poor animal out among the Broadway crowds. Fred arrived just in time to put matters right. He told Adele that if he did not return the innocent goat to the zoo he would have to lose the fifty dollars he had deposited for it.

When Adele did get annoyed, Fred was usually able to smooth her down – and their show gave him a new name for her, 'Funny Face'. She called him 'Sap'.

Only the Astaires could make the work that went into *Funny Face* look as easy as it did. And only the Astaires could perform 'The Babbit and the Bromide' in the run-around and somehow make the scene perfectly intelligible. Others have performed the number in which two people talk rubbish to each other – 'how are you: how're your folks? What's new?' – Fred himself with Gene Kelly, and later, in a solo, Danny Kaye – but none gave it the zest that the Astaires did in *Funny Face*. When Ira Gershwin first produced the lyric, Fred said he understood what a babbit was but didn't have any ideas about a bromide. Vinton Freedley said he knew all about bromides but was mystified about babbits. All the audience knew was that it was a very good number.

''S Wonderful' presented a different kind of problem. One critic complained that it contained an obscene word – 'amorous'. Fortunately, the man's sensitivities were ignored and the word stayed in the song.

Adele became engaged, then broke it. Nevertheless, she and Fred were continuing to lead a very full life. Particularly when Funny Face completed a successful run of 250 performances.

In July 1928, they were weekend guests of the former Princess Xenia of Greece and her husband, William B. Leeds, a millionaire playboy with an estate two miles from New York. As part of the weekend activities, her host took Adele for a jaunt in his shining new speedboat, Fan Tail. It was an idyllic trip, the weather was beautiful, the sea calm. Adele was enjoying everything about it immensely – until, quite suddenly, it all came to a frightening end. As if from nowhere, there was a violent explosion.

A hand, her face and her shoulders were badly burned. Leeds, too, was burned – but less severely. He managed to get the boat to a landing stage and as soon as he had loosely tied up the Fan Tail, lifted Adele to safety.

A local doctor was called and looked over Adele's burns. He ordered that she be taken to Manhatten Hospital without delay. The burns, he decided were 'serious – but not dangerous'. They were serious enough, in fact, to keep her in hospital for several days. The talk on Broadway was that Adele Astaire would never work again. Yet, only a week later, her mother was reporting that she was recovering so nicely that she would leave soon for London and for the run there of *Funny Face*. And to everyone's surprise, she did just that. She arrived in London with Fred as though nothing had happened.

Nobody had any doubts about the way the Astaires were going to be at home in *Funny Face*. They were going to have the top British comic Leslie Henson in the cast with them – taking the role William Kent had had in the New York production – and it all seemed to augur well. The only problem was that the idea seemed to get about that the show was to be called *Sunny Face*.

Funny Face ended its London run after 263 performances – 13 more than in New York, but 63 fewer than had been chalked up by *Lady Be Good* and 155 fewer than *Stop Flirting*. But no one suggested that this was anything but satisfactory.

The society friends they both seemed to accumulate as easily as good notices were as rash with their praise as ever. Among them was a young man to whom Adele had just been introduced, Lord Charles Cavendish, the younger son of the Duke of Devonshire.

It was as natural that someone as effervescent as Adele should be constantly courted as it was for her to want exciting young male company. She was also getting tired of a constant round of Broadway and London shows. When, however, a telegram arrived from Flo Ziegfeld, the most glamorous of all Broadway impresarios, she and Fred both agreed there was nothing to do but accept.

Ziegfeld loved sending telegrams. He also had a passion for Marilyn Miller, the girl who had even seemed to make dish washing sexy when she did it on stage to the tune of 'Look For the Silver Lining'.

His wire to the Astaires appears to have been written in a mood of sheer exhilaration: DEAR FRED AND ADELE: I HAVE WONDERFUL IDEA FOR YOU CO-STARRING WITH MARILYN MILLER – FLO ZIEGFELD.

Alex Aarons was not happy about their leaving the old firm, but Fred convinced him it could be good for them both. It turned out to be just about the most misguided assessment of his professional career. But it makes a good story. The Ziegfeld show was going to be called *Tom, Dick and Harry* and was to open what Flo (in his modesty)

In Smiles, Florenz Ziegfeld teamed Fred and Adele with his current flame, Marilyn Miller, but to no avail. The show was a bomb.

decided would be the most spectacular, the most magnificent, the most elegant theatre in New York. It would be situated slightly off-Broadway, but that did not matter. It could not matter in a theatre to be called the Ziegfeld.

Tom, Dick and Harry was also going to be the most expensive stage production ever to feature the Astaires. Its wages bill alone would total some $40,000 a week, a tenth of which would go to Fred and Adele.

It seemed that this show had everything going for it. Not only did it have the magic of the Astaires and the fame and beauty of Marilyn Miller – to say nothing of the appeal engendered simply by the name Ziegfeld – but it could also boast a score by Vincent Youmans and a book by Noël Coward. Coward's involvement made less of an impact than might be imagined. He had just scored a notable triumph with *Bitter Sweet* which was being produced very successfully at one of Ziegfeld's other theatres, but he was still a very young playwright who was feeling his way.

In the end, the great Ziggy, the man who believed he had his finger firmly on the pulse of Broadway – but whose biggest gift was really the ability to spend money extravagantly – decided he could do without Coward. Instead, he bought the rough outline of Coward's story of a Salvation Army lass – it evoked memories of *The Belle of New York*, a turn-of-the-century musical that Fred himself was to remake as a film nearly thirty years later – and handed it to one William Anthony McGuire. To say the least, that was not an inspired choice. McGuire had something of a reputation as a competent writer of Broadway shows, but his talent did not extend to writing *Tom, Dick and Harry*. The show went on its pre-Broadway run with only half a book and that half was awful. To make things worse, he did not care for the Astaires and they had scarcely any real affection for him. They told Ziegfeld that McGuire was up in the balcony making love to chorus girls when he really ought to have been busy with his typewriter or pencil.

Once the show was due to move into Boston, however, even Ziegfeld had to admit that there was more at stake than just sex. The show was lousy and it seemed there was little that could save it. The title was even worse – but this at least did not present any insurmountable problems. *Tom, Dick and Harry* became *Smiles*. Smiles, however, were not the expressions seen on most faces.

The book was the first thing that had to suffer surgery. In the end, little of the original story remained. And the lyrics of many of the tunes needed to be changed – so Ring Lardner, one of the most brilliant writers of the age, was brought in to provide new words for the songs.

When Ziegfeld decided that a new number might be the only answer to this desperate situation, another writer was called in. Walter Donaldson wrote the tune as a duet for Adele and the then very young Eddie Foy Junior, who, like the Astaires, had been on the vaudeville stage since he was dragged around the tank towns with his father and brothers and sisters as a tiny child, one of the Seven Little Foys. The song was called 'You're Driving Me Crazy'. It was to become one of those classic numbers that now always seem to turn up in a medley of tunes from the twenties. The trouble at the time was that neither Adele nor Foy could remember the words.

They were given just a day to learn the routine, which seemed an impossible task. Foy, however, thought he had the answer. He took some cardboard out of a newly-laundered shirt and on it scribbled Donaldson's lyrics. He then placed it firmly by the footlights. Adele knew of his idea and thought it was just sheer genius. The trouble was that the stagehands were not nearly so enthusiastic as they were – which was hardly surprising since no-one had let them in on the plan. As it was, when at seven p.m., they came on to sweep the stage, they took Foy's shirt cardboard with them.

At eight-thirty, on stage and in the middle of what was going to be the big number, Foy was enthusiastically in his stride. But he could see that Adele was trying to tell him something from the corner of her mouth. Exactly what, he couldn't tell. But there was a song to sing and he was looking forward to doing it. As for Adele, she was always kidding him as she did everyone else, and this time he wasn't going to worry about the risk of being her fall-guy.

The orchestra struck up the introductory music, Foy sidled up to Adele and looked down towards the footlights – and realised what his partner had been trying so hard to tell him.

Adele's answer to the problem was to start to laugh. Foy, ever a showman in the true theatrical tradition, found an instant answer. If he couldn't remember Donaldson's words, he'd invent his own: 'Oh, you're driving me crazy. What'll I do? What'll I do?' To which Adele, adept as she always was, countered: 'Oh, you're going crazy – and so am I. What can we do? What can we do?'

Donaldson was impressed. 'They're very good lyrics,' he told them. 'They're better than the ones I wrote.'

The Band Wagon *was Adele's last show. She and Fred had gone about as far as they could.*

Fred and Adele during The Band Wagon.

"I Love Louisa," a German dialect piece from The Band Wagon.

As Foy now says: 'Oh, it was an awful night. But these things happen in show business.'

All the time that the show wended its unhappy way – there were eight weeks of solid advance booking from the ticket brokers but little more – Fred stayed at the theatre trying to pick up pieces and build something out of them. He kept to himself and rarely went out.

Nothing, it seemed, could protect *Smiles*. Marilyn Miller put the stamp of fate on the whole sad business when she went off to have an operation that still makes people's tongues wag. The official explanation was that she was suffering from sinus trouble, but in truth Flo Ziegfeld looked as worried about her as she was herself.

Meanwhile, Fred was trying at last to find solace outside the theatre. He could be seen going to night clubs – which he still insisted was not his image at all. At the Casino in New York's Central Park, he was in the company of a very pretty girl with hair that almost matched her name. It didn't take long before that name got out. – Ginger Rogers.

It was Alex Aarons who introduced the pair, although he had no thoughts of either professional or romantic entanglements. He was, however, staging a new Gershwin show called *Girl Crazy* and Ginger

Fred found a new partner, Tilly Losch.

With his fiancée, Phyllis Potter.

was his up-and-coming new star, a nineteen-year-old girl from Texas who showed an astonishing talent for making her feet appear weightless. There was, however, a problem. She was basically a Charleston dancer and was finding a number called 'Embraceable You' difficult to perform. Could Fred help? He decided he could and would.

They got on well together after that, and the occasional dates continued. But there was no thought of its blossoming into a full-scale romance. Nor had they considered working together as a team – 'A team? that sounds like a pair of horses,' Fred used to comment. When she later left for Hollywood, they said their farewells and neither had any thought of linking up on the West Coast.

Meanwhile, *Smiles* limped on for the length of the booking agents' commitments and then faded away after sixty-three inglorious performances – two less than had been 'enjoyed' by *The Bunch and Judy*.

It was not the end of the Astaires' interest in the show. They both liked Ziegfeld. Indeed, Adele said she 'just loved Flo'. But in July 1931, they both sued him. They claimed that Ziegfeld owed them $10,000. The money, they said, was salary they had not received. By 27 October 1930, when the show opened, they claimed they should have had a total of $12,000 between them. Instead, they only got $2,000. The case was put to arbitration, but the result was not totally satisfactory to the Astaires. They were awarded $4,000, just one week's salary. Money was important. Both Fred and Adele had lost heavily in the Wall Street crash. But for Adele, the money promised in show business was little more than peanuts compared to the prospects now offered by the future.

She was talking romance.

To a newspaperman, she confided that she thought a woman ought to look for a man who was younger than herself.

What she did not reveal was that in the last few months, Lord Charles Cavendish, seven years her junior, had been becoming a much more noticeable feature of her life than she had previously been willing to allow. He had come to New York as a 'financial apprentice' to join the banking firm of J.P. Morgan and Company and had been seeing a very great deal of Adele.

She told him she couldn't retire on a flop. There would have to be one more good show – and she knew there was one in the offing.

Lyricist Howard Dietz and composer Arthur Schwartz had seen the Astaires at the Ziegfeld Theatre and decided that they wanted to work with them. Max Gordon was anxious to produce an Astaire show and they were delighted to provide the raw material.

As for Fred and Adele, it was not a difficult decision to take. Even Moaning Minnie Fred could see that the show they were offering had alluring possibilities. It was to be called *The Band Wagon* and would be the most exciting of all the Astaire shows – and also the last.

Dietz and Schwartz had achieved near perfection in a musical show and most of what they had planned came off in the way that they wanted it to. As their work on the production seemed to be at an end, Dietz said he still needed a song to be used in a merry-go-round number. In a matter of seconds, he scribbled on a sheet of yellow paper the opening lines of a tune that was to show Fred Astaire at his most versatile best. It was called 'I Love Louisa'.

There was something more exciting and more elegant still in a dance without words in the show – although Dietz had written a set of lyrics for it immediately after picking up a book from his personal library called *Dancers in the Dark*. Dietz called his song after this title and told Schwartz about his inspiration. The composer rushed home in the early hours of the morning and played the melody he had devised for the title over and over again – because he had no manuscript paper handy and was frightened of forgetting it. The tune, he admits, took him a matter of minutes to write.

From the moment that Astaire danced it with Tilly Losch, 'Dancing in the Dark' became a classic.

Adele, meanwhile, contemplated the effect that the success of *The Band Wagon* was likely to have on her career. She decided that the time had finally come. This was the peak. It was the right moment to retire. The first person to be told had to be Lord Charles Cavendish – Charlie. At a party, after a single drink, she proposed.

Fred aboard the S.S. Homeric, *returning from England in 1932, after a successful London run of* The Gay Divorce.

July 12, 1933. The wedding portrait of Mr. and Mrs. Fred Astaire. Next to Phyllis are her uncle, Henry Worthington Bull, and Judge Selah B. Strong.

It was just one drink at the '21' that signalled the end of one of the most successful Broadway partnerships in history. Adele and Charles Cavendish were at the club, which had by now become New York's most fashionable speakeasy, and the one drink had apparently gone to her head – she hardly ever drank at all and the occasions when she did seem to have gone on the record with some extremely notable consequences.

'You know, we get on so well,' she told him, 'I think we ought to get married.'

'Righto,' he answered. The following morning, Lord Charles rang Adele at her Park Avenue apartment: 'You proposed to me last night and I accepted. If you don't accept *me*, I'll sue you for breach of promise.'

The next person to be told was Fred – who reacted with a kiss and his best wishes. He always knew the moment was going to come sooner or later and he also knew that she was unlikely to marry another performer. The chances of her remaining as part of the team, and whether it sounded like a pair of horses or not, that is precisely what they were, were always remote. Now she confirmed it.

Both determined there would be no sad farewells. But Adele now admits her brother was frustrated at the thought of having to make it on his own. He had physically pushed his elder sister into the limelight to the extent that many reviewers had made her the senior partner. Now he was going to be put to the test. But Adele said she had little doubt he would make it without her. The way he and Tilly Losch performed together night after night in *The Band Wagon* in scenes in which she herself was not involved confirmed this.

Fred was not, however, going to be thrown in at the deep end immediately. Adele promised she would see out the Broadway run of the show and would start the road tour with the company, too.

Adele kept her word and stayed with the show throughout its New York run of 260 performances and saw it through the beginning of the tour, too.

But on an evening in March 1932 at the Illinois Theatre in Chicago, the big breakup came. With tears running down her cheeks, Adele left the theatre that night – and in more ways than one. It was the last time she appeared in *The Band Wagon* and also her last professional appearance on any stage at all.

Vera Marsh took over Adele's role and found out just how difficult it could be to step into her shoes. She was a good little dancer, but the public couldn't accept anyone but Fred's sister teasing and dancing with him.

Very soon after the Cavendishes set up home at Lismore, Fred paid them a visit to offer personally his brotherly good wishes for their future happiness. He also had something to tell them. He was in love himself.

Fred with Claire Luce in The Gay Divorcee, *a smash in both New York and London. (Where it was called* The Gay Divorce.)

39

The quiet, hard-working business-comes-first Fred had spent a Sunday afternoon at the private golf course of a member of the Vanderbilt family. At lunch he had been introduced to Mrs Phyllis Potter, then at the tail end of an unhappy marriage to a Wall Street stockbroker.

She divorced her husband, Eliphalet Nott Potter the Third at Reno in January 1932 and was granted custody of her three-year-old son, Eliphalet Nott Potter, the Fourth – who happily was called Peter. But she only had the boy with her for nine months of the year. The rest of the time he had to spend with his father. Phyllis was not satisfied with this arrangement. She believed that the boy needed to be with her throughout the year, and until that was settled, there could be no new serious entanglement for her.

On his way back from Ireland, Fred met up with Phyllis again – but she held out little hope of marrying him. The problems seemed too big.

There was only one thing for Fred to do, both agreed, concentrate on the new show that was to mark the emergence of the solo Fred Astaire, with the aid of a score by Cole Porter. One of its backers was to be Fred's old friend Jock Whitney. It was, Astaire decided, going to have to be a weather vane show, on it would depend the whole future of his career as a dancer and actor. This would prove whether he could exist on stage without Adele. It was a daunting proposition, but it had to be accepted.

Claire Luce, a delightful blonde dancer, was given the role that Adele would have had. The show was *Gay Divorce* – based on an unproduced play by Hartley Manners that had been scheduled for the stage many times but had never managed to get off the ground.

The press didn't know what to make of Fred Astaire as a single. Those who made up their minds were lukewarm, to say the least. One reviewer wrote: 'Astaire stops every now and then to look off-stage towards the wings – as if hoping his titled sister would come out and rescue him.'

People thought *The Gay Divorce* was all right, too. After a time, even Brooks Atkinson, the principal Butcher of Broadway, offered what might have been thought a slightly back-handed compliment. He wrote: 'In the refulgent Claire Luce, Fred Astaire has found a partner who can match him step for step and who flies over the furniture in his company without missing a beat. As a solo dancer, Mr Astaire stamps out his accents with that lean, nervous agility that distinguishes his craftsmanship and he has invented turns that abound in graphic portraiture.'

Now, however, came the rub. Atkinson added:

'But some of us cannot help feeling that the joyousness of the Astaire team is missing now that the team has parted.'

Fred was also thinking more about his relationship with Phyllis.

On 11 July 1933 it appeared that things had come to a head. Phyllis left her home on East 62nd Street and went before Supreme Court

Justice Selah B. Strong in Brooklyn. She declared on oath that she did not intend to marry Fred Astaire until she was satisfied she would be allowed to devote all of her attention to her child. In short, she was asking for full-time custody of Peter.

Both she and her uncle, Mr Bull, whose address was given as Islip, Long Island, testified. Asked about her plans with Fred, she said she had not given him any definite answer – because she was not sure that marriage would allow her to carry out her full duties to her child. Judge Strong was suitably impressed. The following day, he granted Phyllis custody of Peter for eleven months, instead of nine, and she was allowed to take the boy anywhere she liked. The father could visit him whenever he wished, too.

The decision reached, the Judge just took off his robes. Then, when they went into his private chambers, Phyllis told him: 'I've decided to marry Mr Astaire right away, now that I know that Peter's future is assured.'

There was a hurried discussion and the Judge put on his robes once more. In the court library he performed a wedding ceremony. Phyllis was wearing a light coloured summer dress and Fred, who had taken the precaution of procuring a licence just in case, a grey business suit.

After the ceremony, Mr and Mrs Astaire posed for photographers in one of the court building's corridors, and went back to Fred's apartment at 875 Park Avenue – where he immediately button-holed the doorman. 'Aw gee,' he shouted ecstatically, 'she's married me,' and then he thumped the unsuspecting man in livery on the chest. They couldn't afford to take off more than that one day because Fred had commitments on the West Coast. He had finally decided that he was now going to worry less about the stage and would try his luck in Hollywood. More important, Hollywood had decided to try Fred Astaire.

Any discussion of Fred and Phyllis leads inevitably to a mass of clichés. They were the happiest couple in Hollywood. Their's wasn't a filmland marriage. They knocked on the head the old adage about the inevitability of divorce among anyone in the showbiz set. It was all true. And one reason was that they went to Hollywood because it offered not a new way of life, but just a new career prospect. Neither dared speculate that Fred had made his last Broadway appearance, but he had.

Their one-day honeymoon was spent cruising down the Hudson River in the yatch *Captiva*, lent to them by a friend. The following day they went flying down to California to make a movie called *Flying Down To Rio*. When they arrived in Hollywood after a twenty-six-hour flight – it was Fred's first time in a commercial aircraft – the film city was as anxious to meet the wife of the Broadway star as it was to see Astaire himself.

One writer observed that Phyllis was 'undeniably pretty – not in the Hollywood manner, but rather in the manner of those tailored-hat ads in the smart fashion papers. She's smaller and slighter even than Fred, about Adele's size – but with none of Adele's gay insouciance.'

The contract for *Flying Down to Rio* was with RKO Radio pictures – recently formed by an amalgam of the old Keith-Orpheum Circuits which Fred and Adele had known so well in their vaudeville days. As far as RKO were concerned, it was a gamble, which they desperately needed to come off. The studio was mortgaged up to its collective eyeballs. In fact, there were two Wall Street bankers who were acting as receivers for the company. One false step and it was ready for final liquidation.

If Fred could come up trumps, the wolves could be sent scurrying from the door.

Before work on the picture got under way, Fred had a chore to do. It amounted, in fact, to a dress rehearsal for *Flying Down to Rio* and for his entire Hollywood career. MGM had offered him a guest appearance in the new film they were preparing for Joan Crawford and a rather awkward young man with big ears, Clark Gable. It was called *Dancing Lady*. His name in the film was – Fred Astaire. He played the star of the Broadway show in which Miss Crawford was being given the big break – later Claire Luce was to claim that she saw amazing similarities between the story and her own history of breaking into show business. Gable was the hard-bitten producer of the show, Franchot Tone his rival for Miss Crawford's romantic affections, Robert Benchley was a newspaper columnist, and also in the cast were Eve Arden, the Three Stooges and even Nelson Eddy singing at the film's end.

Gable didn't like being made subordinate to La Crawford in the billing and had a row with Louis B. Mayer over it. The result was that Mayer decided to punish him – by handing the erring star to the run-down studio operating from an area of Hollywood known as Poverty

With Joan Crawford in his first motion picture, Dancing Lady.

Row. The company was Columbia Pictures. The film was Frank Capra's *It Happened One Night*, which literally became over-laden with Oscars.

In *Dancing Lady* Fred danced in top hat and tails and when he made his first entrance he told Phyllis he thought he looked like a knife. But she told him he looked lovely and that was praise enough. His scene lasted just four minutes fifty seconds, but there could never have been a more important four minutes fifty seconds in his entire career. They proved that not only could Fred be a dominant film personality, but that he liked the medium, too.

He wasn't the star of *Flying Down To Rio*. In fact, no one could be sure for long who were the stars. Helen Broderick, then a light comedy favourite, was first mentioned as a star. So was Arline Judge. Joel McRea was listed, too. But they all dropped out. Finally Dolores Del Rio and Gene Raymond were brought in.

Fred and director Mark Sandrich clowning on the set of the film The Gay Divorcee.

As the juvenile female lead, the studio selected . . . Ginger Rogers, and to play opposite her, Fred Astaire. But they forgot to tell either of them about it. Fred said he was delighted to meet Ginger again, but was totally taken aback when the announcement was first made. Ginger just heard he was on the lot, but knew nothing more.

The girl who began her career when she was spotted by Eddie Cantor – and then sent by him on a tour of New York theatres – had gone on to unexpected heights in *Girl Crazy* and then had a $1,000-a-week role in Pathe's *The Tip Off*. Now, she saw she was already an important Hollywood property. But she was plainly not important enough to be told with whom she was to play.

Fred said he just happened to hear someone say: 'Let's get Fred and Ginger together.' Certainly, neither of them imagined it would blossom into anything more.

They were helped by a score by Vincent Youmans, who seemed a lot happier than he had been in *Smiles* and rightfully so. His most inspired part of the score was the big production number 'The Carioca' in which Fred and Ginger showed how a couple could dance, not cheek to cheek, but forehead to forehead.

Astaire and Rogers were very much the second leads in the picture – Fred playing merely the best friend of Gene Raymond, a band leader and pilot who was in love with the beautiful Miss Del Rio. Ginger was the vocalist in Raymond's orchestra.

The director of *Flying Down To Rio* was Thornton Freeland. Early on, during one of Fred's solo numbers, he carefully drew a chalk line on the studio floor.

'Whatever you do,' he instructed Astaire, 'don't go beyond these lines. Otherwise, you'll be out of frame.'

Fred had only gone through half his number when he was completely carried away by the experience. He concentrated so hard on the steps he had to do for the routine that he completely forgot about the chalked line.

44

'That was a helluva lot of good work for nothing,' Freeland told him. 'Didn't you hear me call "Cut"? You kept crossing that chalked line so many times that you might have been having a skipping game. Now, when you're ready, we'll take it again. . . .'

'The Carioca' took, it was estimated, a hundred hours to rehearse and lasted about four minutes on screen.

By the time the film was over Fred did some careful reckoning. He now worked out he had danced a total of 100,000 miles in his career.

Fred was to say that he learned a great deal about filming techniques when he made *Flying Down To Rio*. Possibly his biggest single gain from the production came with a lanky young man who bore an astonishing resemblance to Fred himself, in build and appearance, in voice and in dedication to the dance as not merely an art work but as a serious labour.

He was Hermes Pan – the surname, an abbreviation for the Greek Panagiotopulos. He was six years younger than Fred and had been born in Tennessee, which as far as the casual listener was concerned, was responsible for the only real difference in their accents. A dancer himself, he was now working on the RKO lot as an assistant dance director. When Fred was finally installed in the company, the two were introduced to each other and Pan was asked to give Fred any

45

help he could. He not only helped on the dance floor, but it was to be the beginning of a lasting friendship between them.

Now, with the filming over, Fred had an obligation to meet – two obligations, in fact: Phyllis had not yet had the real honeymoon he had promised her. And he was contracted to do *Gay Divorce* in London. He decided that both commitments could be fulfilled together, and with a visit to 'Delly' thrown in at the same time.

Once their bags were packed, the Astaires ran round to their friends' houses, saying goodbye.

Fred told Ginger that it had been a useful experiment, but dancing would never catch on on the screen. In a studio executive's office, he suggested that perhaps it wouldn't be a bad idea if the dance routines were cut out completely. No one could be found who did agree – so Fred suggested remaking them. This time, he was shown the door and told to come back when he had finished in London. The men at RKO had ideas that might make him feel better.

Adele actually heard Fred before she saw him. Soon after arriving in London, the BBC invited him to do a radio show – something that he avoided whenever he could, because he considered himself principally a visual entertainer. But the BBC shared the view of the top song writers of the age that Fred could sing their work more faithfully than almost any other performer.

She was not in the audience the night the show opened at the Palace Theatre on 2 November 1933 because a few days earlier she had given birth prematurely to a baby girl. The baby died almost immediately. Adele was both heartbroken and ill for some time.

But the people in the theatre the evening of the London opening knew only that it was yet another great occasion. Among those in the

In 1933, Fred got a new dancing partner. Her name — Ginger Rogers.

Fred and Hermes Pan, his long-time dance director and close friend, work out a dance routine during the filming of Roberta.

A scene from The Gay Divorcee. *Left to right: Alice Brady, Edward Everett Horton, Erik Rhodes, Ginger Rogers, Fred Astaire.*

Dancing to Cole Porter's "Night and Day" in The Gay Divorcee.

stalls was Prince George. When it came to the routine in which Fred and Clare Luce had to dance over the furniture, the thing Astaire feared most of all happened, they fell.

Miss Luce fell so badly that she damaged her hip. It was eventually to lead her to a lengthy stay in hospital and before long mean the end of her dancing career, but she got up and in great pain did the dance again. What is more, she kept on doing it throughout the run of the show.

Fred had no idea how serious her injuries were, although he was very solicitous about her well-being. His main concern was whether

or not he had made a fool of himself. Nobody mentioned the fall. It wasn't even reported in the following morning's papers.

Several weeks after the opening, Adele was well enough to see the show at the Palace. She was treated regally – flowers, speeches and a mass of adoration for 'Funny Face' from 'Sap'. It was the first time she had ever seen him from the other side of the footlights, a chastening experience. It was also, she said, the first time she realised that her brother had sex-appeal – although in many ways the worried look on his face reminded her of the wrinkles that drooped from one of her pet dachshund's eyes.

With his mother, Mrs. Ann Astaire.

Fred, however, would never believe anyone who assured him he was a great success. He worried that he wasn't doing well enough in *Gay Divorce*, and when Walter promised him that the people out front were not applauding simply to be polite, he worried that there might be another fall on stage.

Nothing bothered him more, however, than the thought of what was happening in Hollywood. Before leaving for London he and Phyllis had started settling down to life on the West Coast and were enjoying the relaxed way in which even stars were able to have something resembling a private life. At that stage, Fred certainly did not feel committed to a career in films, but he was, as always, committed to doing a satisfactory job. And he did not yet know just how satisfactory *Flying Down To Rio* had been. He hadn't seen a preview because he left the country before the film was ready. So now every message from America seemed as if it might be a potential threat to his whole career.

Every time a cable arrived from the States it was Phyllis or Adele who would have to open it – in case it contained a message of doom to Fred Astaire, film actor.

When the prognosis finally came, it was greeted with undisguised relief. Pandro S. Berman whose first name was an abbreviation for Pandrovich sent Fred the wire which confirmed he had more than made the grade:

FLYING DOWN TO RIO COLOSSAL SUCCESS STOP OFFERING SEVEN YEAR CONTRACT STOP MAKE SURE FILM RIGHTS GAY DIVORCE STOP REPRESENTATIVE WITH NEGOTIATIONS RIGHT ON WAY TO YOU.

Berman, son of Russian-Jewish immigrants, was still in his twenties, but was already regarded as one of the top whizz-kids in Hollywood. He was to RKO what Thalberg represented to MGM, the boy genius whose ideas just had to be followed through.

There was talk in London that Fred was about to make a film with the darling of the British musical comedy stage, Jessie Matthews. Isabel N. Gordon wrote to the *New York Times* from Mount Vernon, New York, protesting.

'I want to say, as one of the vast American theatre-going public, that the present Fred Astaire–Ginger Rogers suits me to a T. Moreover, I imagine my choice is representative of the majority of the film-going public in this country.'

There had been only one Astaire–Rogers film so far, but RKO had insisted there were going to be more and Miss Gordon wanted to be sure they kept their word. Fred, the studio announced, was going back to work just as soon as the London run of *Gay Divorce* ended. But London was making it very clear that it did not want the run to end. It was Fred's first show in the British capital for five years and the citizens of the city were treasuring every moment of it.

But the end of *Gay Divorce* had to come. After 108 performances, the curtain closed for the last time – both for the show and for Fred Astaire. He would never appear, full time, in a live theatre again.

Fred was still in London when a newspaper revealed that his next film partner was going to be the British actress Diana Wynyard. The picture was going to be the screen version of *Gay Divorce*.

The story, like so many about stars who were the public idols of the day, was only partly right: *Gay Divorce* was such a success that it was indeed going to be filmed, but Diana Wynyard had not been selected for the role.

RKO, in fact, couldn't get Fred back to work quickly enough, and that meant back to work with Ginger. Miss Rogers was less than ecstatic about being told to make another musical and Fred thought he was being saddled with the inevitability of always being part of a 'team of horses' again. But he relented.

Gay Divorce appealed to him as much as it did to Pan Berman. He had developed the same sort of affection for 'Night and Day' now as had the audiences who cheered it both on Broadway and in London. But he did have those reservations about co-starring with Ginger. And not just simply because he didn't want a regular partner. She wasn't English and without an English girl to sing and dance with, he thought, *Gay Divorce* wouldn't work. Berman's view of this was that the audiences 'didn't give a hoot'.

Astaire and Rogers could be persuaded. Louis Brock, the producer of *Flying Down To Rio*, could not. He didn't like the story and didn't want to make it into a film. 'Right,' said Berman, 'if you won't make it – I will.' And he did, and as a result was to be credited with the biggest success RKO had yet had.

The Hays Office didn't approve of a divorce ever being considered gay – it was just that Mr Family Man American was expected to regard a divorce as a tragedy that was a solemn occasion for all concerned. But an alternative title was found without too much difficulty and the clean-up campaigners were immediately satisfied. If it were called 'The Gay Divor*cee*', they reckoned, there would be very little difference in the box office appeal – few of the people who had either seen or wanted to see the show would notice the difference – and, strangely, no one could see any moral objection to a divorcee being gay if the action itself remained tragic.

Of the music, only 'Night and Day' was considered memorable enough to be repeated on film. So it stayed, with Fred using most of the original steps he had done with Claire Luce. But Cole Porter was not involved in any of the other numbers. The rest of the score which now only amounted to three songs, was provided by Con Conrad and Harry Revel, with lyrics by Herb Magidson and Mack Gordon.

Apart from 'Night and Day', which in early talkie terms was a sensation, there was only one really big number in the *Gay Divorcee* film – 'The Continental', which had Astaire and Rogers sweeping through a chorus that managed to turn a black and white film into a riot of colour. The first male dancers to be seen were in white tails, while the girls with them wore black. Behind these was another group of about twenty dancers with the men in black and the girls in white.

At the back of these was still a third group where the colours, this time, were mixed. The male chorus dancers wore white jackets and black trousers while the girls had white dresses with black trains-cum-sashes. The effect was stunning. And so was the dancing of 'The Continental' by Astaire and Rogers.

Usually, the music in a picture was closely guarded until the film was ready for release – that way it could be relied upon to do some good, publicising the film. But 'The Continental' escaped. Somehow, the dance bands got hold of it and it was being played all over America before the film was released.

The work on *The Gay Divorcee* was worth every dripping shirt and each salty tear. The public loved it, and Adele said it made her realise that she must have been holding Fred back all the years they had worked together.

Immediately after *Gay Divorcee*, Ginger Rogers was assigned to other pictures. She was told, however, that there would be more Astaire vehicles on the way – and, like it or not, she was expected to do them. She didn't like it, but the choice was not hers; it is frequently forgotten that throughout the whole period in which she and Fred were working together, she was making other films in between, sometimes as many as three a year. They were, however, eminently forgettable.

Fred managed to take time off in between pictures – playing golf with Phyllis, who proved to be a player of championship standard, and going deep-sea fishing with her. She could bring in a giant marlin more than three times her own ninety pound weight as easily as lesser mortals could carry shopping baskets.

Fred, meanwhile, was back at work at RKO with Ginger, with Pandro S. Berman as producer and Hermes Pan as his dance director, and working harder than almost any other performer would have thought possible. He was now so fussy about everything working out perfectly that he did not even trust other people to nail the taps on to the toes and heels of his dancing shoes, so he did this bit of cobbling himself.

The new film was *Roberta*, an adaptation of the stage play which had marked the big-time debut of a young comedian called Bob Hope. It was centred around a fashion house. In the film Fred played Hope's part. He was a band leader, Ginger a secretary. Astaire's real life close friend Randolph Scott was on hand too, as a country bumpkin who takes over the couturier's establishment.

The strange thing about *Roberta* was that, despite the overwhelming success of *Gay Divorcee*, Astaire and Rogers were no more the stars of the new picture than they had been in *Flying Down To Rio*. Berman decided to use the elegant Irene Dunne in the film as the principal brains behind the fashion house – because at the time she represented even bigger box office pulling power than either Fred or Ginger.

In one scene, Miss Dunne had to lean forward to examine a button on the dress worn by a model. Fred thought she was showing too much cleavage and asked her if it was really in the best of taste. 'I thought he was too stuffy for words,' she says now. 'But afterwards I thought he was right.'

An important plus in *Roberta's* favour was the score – this time by Jerome Kern. Another, which seemed a lot less notable at the time, was the appearance of a young lady called Lucille Ball.

Few of the songs in the original Broadway show were transferred to the screen – with Kern's finest number sung first by Irene Dunne and then reprised as a dance routine in all its considerable glory by Astaire and Rogers. It was 'Smoke Gets In Your Eyes'.

Two other tunes were added by Kern himself, both of them important in any song history of the century – 'I Won't Dance', and 'Lovely To Look At' which was to become the title of a later remake of the *Roberta* story. That song presented a few worries to Pandro Berman who said it was much too short. 'That's all I have to say,' replied Kern, leaving absolutely nothing more, in fact, to be said.

Fred danced both on-camera and off- for his incredible taps had to be heard as well as seen. It was the hardest and least rewarding part of his screen work, but recording the sound of his dancing had to be done and as usual he had to do it the Astaire way. Other dancers might have been satisfied with their taps recorded by a drummer using coconut shells, but Fred had to do his as though there were a thousand people in the studio watching him. If he could spot a single beat that failed to match the action on screen, that and all the other taps would be repeated until everything was perfect.

Ginger, however, was not quite so fussy. Nobody expected her to be able to work with that sort of precision, so nobody asked. As a result, every Rogers step was later repeated by Hermes Pan. With a pair of earphones on his head and his loudest tap shoes on his feet, Pan repeated each step that Ginger had done on the screen. So whenever Ginger is seen dancing in those films, it is Hermes Pan's shoes you hear, not hers. It was rather like a vocalist dubbing a tune for a non-singing actor, except that there was no optical illusion about her performances. Certainly, the effect of seeing Pan dance with Fred wouldn't have been anything like as stunning.

If the amount of work put into a number had any bearing on the results, *Roberta* had to be brilliant. There was a solid nine-week period of rehearsals before shooting started – much of it all by Fred on his own; he didn't take off a Saturday, a Sunday or even a public holiday. Rehearsals covered the days of Thanksgiving, Christmas and New Year. On each of these, he telephoned Hermes Pan in the morning and suggested they get together for a couple of hours that afternoon 'to rehearse some more'.

For *Roberta*, he rehearsed dance routines that came to him before he had any idea of the music they would accompany. The steps were planned two weeks before Kern delivered the score.

The songwriter, who was not usually given to ungrudging admiration of another man's capabilities, was stunned by Fred's innate musical sense. On one occasion, to prove a point, Fred danced through

Astaire and Rogers.

53

Kern's Beverly Hills house as the composer watched the procession from room to room, wide-eyed and incredulous.

Every step was rehearsed day after day from nine in the morning until six in the evening – with Ginger turning up for work in slacks and Fred dressing as informally as he always did at these times. It was difficult to imagine how different everything would be when she was in her flowing ball gown and he in his white tie and tails. But Fred and Pan knew – and Ginger took their word for it.

Filming complete, Fred took off as usual with Phyllis to play golf and then went deep sea fishing in the Lower Gulf of California with their friend Randolph Scott. All the time that Fred was away, he seemed to be worrying as much about his newly-finished picture as he was about getting a hole-in-one or catching a 150-lb marlin.

Early on Fred set a pattern to which he would religiously keep: he avoided going to previews of his pictures and there were, in fact, some films he couldn't bring himself to see until years after they were made. If he had gone to see *Roberta* at the preview stage, 'Moaning Minnie' might have stopped moaning. No one could pretend it was a great film; the plot and much of the acting was pedestrian. But Astaire and Rogers stole it for every minute they were on the screen.

The press had no doubts whatever.

Said the *New York Times*: 'The Kublai Khans at RKO have erected a bright and shimmering pleasure dome. The work is a model of urbanity in the musical films and Mr Astaire, the debonair master of light comedy and the dance, is its chief ornament.

'To watch him skipping on effortless cat's feet across a dance floor is to experience one of the major delights of the contemporary cinema.'

The only fault in the production was that Fred 'and his excellent partner, Miss Rogers, cannot be dancing during every minute of it'.

It was enough to make anyone connected with Fred Astaire feel marvellously contented. But not Fred Astaire himself.

RKO and almost everyone else in Hollywood were by now convinced that there was an Astaire–Rogers bandwagon in full motion and with nothing to stop it. Fred, however, needed a great deal more convincing. Not even the record-breaking box-office figures assuaged his concern.

The future of the sort of films he was making was even more difficult to predict. Just how long would audiences accept the slightly abrasive Miss Rogers constantly mistaking Fred's true intentions?

The dancing was more difficult to plan every time. He and Pan had learned a number of lessons, particularly as far as placing the camera to the best advantage was concerned. You couldn't photograph dancers in the way you could other performers – audiences had to see their feet as well as their faces, but not always at the same time. The art was being able to decide which camera angle matched which beat of the music and which tap of the stars' feet.

All that dexterity and technical skill was going to be needed when a small, desperately shy man with shiny black hair walked on to the

THEY'RE DANCING CHEEK-TO-CHEEK AGAIN!

FRED **ASTAIRE**
GINGER **ROGERS**

in

TOP HAT

MUSIC AND LYRICS BY
IRVING BERLIN

WITH
EDWARD EVERETT HORTON
HELEN BRODERICK
ERIK RHODES · ERIC BLORE
Directed by MARK SANDRICH
A PANDRO S. BERMAN Production

Top Hat established once and for all the Astaire–Rogers style: white tie and tails for Fred, the latest in high fashion for Ginger.

RKO lot and started pounding on an upright piano as though it were a punchbag. Every now and again, he would reach for a lever under the keyboard and attempt to play the tune again – always entirely on the black notes.

His name was Irving Berlin, and playing the piano in the key of F sharp was the only way he knew. He had to use a battered upright – he called it his 'Buick' – because that was the only one that could be fitted with a lever which would automatically change key for him, like a gear stick on a car.

What he was pounding out for the stars and the assembled company of RKO executives was a score that he figured summed up Fred Astaire to the bottom of his impeccably pressed trousers. To match Astaire's dancing, the studio had retained the most successful songwriter in musical history, the Russian-born Jewish cantor's son who with the name of a German city had become the unofficial American poet laureate in song. The film was going to become Astaire's trademark, the archetype vehicle for what was to be regarded as a typical Astaire performance in a perfect Rogers–Astaire mould – *Top Hat*.

Berlin has said he would never have written some of his most successful numbers if he hadn't had Fred Astaire to write for. Certainly he would never have written 'Top Hat, White Tie and Tails'. Neither would we probably have had 'Cheek to Cheek', 'Isn't This A Lovely

Day' and the sort of number the public hoped would return in *Top Hat*– the new dance performed by Fred and Ginger as part of a spectacular which this time was called *The Piccolino*.

Before the filming started, the studio prop department worked out, as they always did, exactly what would be needed to make the picture complete. Among them, a hansom cab, a street light, a sword and a collection of canes.

'How many do we need?' asked the prop manager. 'About a dozen,' Hermes Pan recommended. To be on the safe side he ordered thirteen. As the day went on, no one was sweating more blood than the props man. Fred was unhappy with the way the number was shaping up. Every time he felt really depressed about it all, he snapped a cane.

During this sequence he was joined by a man who was fairly used to appearing before the cameras himself, if usually with a somewhat more lethal weapon in his hands. He was James Cagney. Cagney watched one cane after the other being snapped – one, two, three . . . he was actually on cane number eight, when Fred finally decided he would be happy to see the rushes. The take he chose was the first of forty in which he had performed, long before any of the other canes were brought into use. He decided to dedicate the scene to Cagney –, and to suggest that before long they should make a film together. If they waited till they were too old, they would both regret it. They both have.

The *Top Hat* number was not the only one to bring problems. The innocent-sounding, romantic, beautiful and feathery 'Cheek to Cheek' was much more difficult. And it was the feathers that gave everyone who had anything to do with the scene the biggest headache of all.

As always, the dance routine for 'Cheek to Cheek' had been meticulously rehearsed. Berlin saw it, so did Hermes Pan and so did the rehearsal pianist Hal Borne. All the other people involved in the picture were banned from the sanctuary of the Astaire-Rogers presence during rehearsals.

And as always, too, Ginger, in slacks, sat in her chair watching Fred and Pan chart the dance numbers on the rehearsal room blackboard. Just occasionally, she might make a suggestion of her own, but she didn't pretend to be technically minded and left the work of planning the 'battle' to Fred and his choreographer.

Nobody, however, anticipated what would happen when Fred – wearing the first of his stiff shirts under his thick black tail coat – and Ginger in her ballgown, came on to the studio floor and started dancing before the cameras.

To coin a phrase, the feathers flew. They flew into Fred's eyes, on to his shoulders, into his mouth and lodged unhappily, in his ears. Fred kept sneezing, much to his and everybody else's amusement. The names he called the dress and its feathers hadn't been heard coming out of the Astaire lips since his days on Broadway.

Once the commotion had died down, Fred and Pan laughed themselves into composing a parody to Berlin's 'Cheek to Cheek' lyrics – a rare indulgence on the songwriter's part if he ever knowingly

allowed it: Berlin, who used to print instructions on his sheet music forbidding parodies, has been known to take people to court for less.

On this occasion, the Berlin line beginning 'Heaven, I'm in heaven. . .' became 'Feathers, I hate feathers . . .'

The story was as weak as ever, but who cared whether or not Ginger did think Fred had an affliction that made him dance on the floor of his hotel suite – which conveniently just happened to be above hers?

The big white sets that became an RKO trademark almost as recognisable as Fred and Ginger themselves, were in evidence and so were the huge ultra-modern settings for the big production numbers. In *Top Hat*, Astaire and Edward Everett Horton fly to Venice and land their seaplane at just the spot where Ginger is waiting for someone else.

The usual case of mistaken identity combined with the usual insults from Ginger. And as usual, too, they dance off at the end in each other's arms. Once more, there was also Lucille Ball in a now-you-see-her-now-you-don't role.

Fred and Ginger always went their separate ways outside the studio. They had not socialised with each other since those early dates at Manhatten night clubs. Once in Hollywood, Fred and Phyllis had set up a home that intentionally excluded as much of the show business world as possible. They rarely went out to parties and if they did, it was with their own small coterie of friends, which included David Niven and Randolph Scott but few other actors. Fred and Ginger got on well together, but they were content to say goodnight to each other at the end of a day's filming and then, when a picture was finally completed, *au revoir* until the next one – always with Ginger for her own reasons hoping there would not be a next one.

Top Hat opened at New York's Radio City Music Hall – which gives some idea of the importance of the picture – to an incredible reaction from the public. Almost every performance was greeted with thunderous applause from the audience.

The press was equally enthusiastic. *The New York Times* said of the picture: 'Irving Berlin has written some charming melodies for the photoplay and the best of the current cinema teams does them agile justice on the dance floor.'

Top Hat looked like an expensive film by 1935 standards and there were worries about ever getting back the $600,000 the studio had invested, particularly since both Fred and Irving Berlin were in on ten per cent of the profits. (Ginger had her more modest contract salary and was about to be directed to another film.)

In the end, the picture grossed three million dollars.

Meanwhile, the family was due to expand. Both Phyllis and Adele were pregnant.

In September 1935, Adele gave birth to twin boys. But again, both died. This was now the saddest point in her whole life. The happy-go-lucky clown of the family was distraught. She now knew that she would never have what she wanted most, a child.

While Phyllis waited for what Reuter's newsagency described as her 'happy event', Fred was trying out a new medium and was not over impressed. He was the link-man – cum-singer in a radio series for 'Lucky Strike' cigarettes called the Hit Parade. It was a superb opportunity to plug *Top Hat*, to sing Irving Berlin's songs and the other numbers that were selling in the record stores. He also danced a bit, too – at the end of the show on a tiny dance floor with a special mike at foot level to pick up the taps. It was while relaxing that he thought up his own music. He had worked on a number of tunes since his first was published in 1924. Several of them were published and had sold quite well. For 'Tappin' The Time' in 1927 his old friend Jock Whitney had written the lyrics. 'Blue Without You' and 'More and More' came in 1930 and 'Not My Girl' in 1935. But in 1936 was the real block buster songwriting year. He had 'Just One More Dance, Madame' (for which the very experienced Dave Dreyer supplied the lyrics with Paul Francis Webster); 'I'll Never Let You Go', (Dreyer again with Jack Ellis), and what was to prove the biggest success of his life – 'I'm Building Up To An Awful Let Down'.

Johnny Mercer collaborated with Astaire on that and the result was a vocalisation of the sheer poetry Astaire had previously seemed to reserve for his dancing. The song got to the top of the hit parade and for Fred it seemed to justify the membership he had taken out some time before in ASCAP – the American Society of Composers, Authors and Publishers.

Irving Berlin had to be at the top of the list of Astaire's favourite songwriters. After the almost unbelievable success of *Top Hat*, Pandro S. Berman booked him for the next Rogers–Astaire film, a movie in which Fred wore bell-bottoms as well as the expected top hat, white tie and tails.

The picture was *Follow The Fleet*, a remake of a musical filmed only six years before as *Hit The Deck* – which itself had been based on a 1925 vintage silent movie called *Shore Leave*. In this new version Randolph Scott appeared with his old friend.

The film wasn't Fred's usual image at all. He could actually be seen chewing gum, and when he gave the embarrassed little bronchial laugh that turns up in all the Astaire films – and, indeed, in any conversation with Fred, even today – it was usually in the midst of a diction that sounded totally strange coming from his mouth.

Ginger is a dance hall queen and Fred the fellow she used to dance with, who decides to join the Navy and who in reality would rather lead a band – to coin a title of one of the songs in the film. He also leads the chorus in singing 'We Saw The Sea', all about the joys of world travel.

But although 'We Saw The Sea' went to the top of the 1936 hit parade, it was the numbers with Rogers which, as usual, were the show stoppers – including 'I'm Putting All My Eggs In One Basket' and 'Let's Face the Music and Dance'. That was yet another classic which easily could have been a new signature tune for Fred any time he wanted

to discard 'Top Hat, White Tie and Tails'. But this was also to give Fred problems – it was shot about fifteen times yet it was the first take that was used.

Lucille Ball had yet another microscopic role in *Follow The Fleet* and the singing trio included the blonde who at the time seemed destined to do nothing more than smile in Fred Astaire–Ginger Rogers pictures, Betty Grable. No one had yet begun to guess at the potential those legs of hers offered for cheering up the boys in World War Two.

There were nearly as many costume problems in *Follow The Fleet* as there had been in *Top Hat*. Except that in the new film, the feathers were, by some kind of poetic justice, replaced by what appeared to be lead weights. Ginger wore a metallic skirt for the 'Let's Face The Music And Dance' number, a garment that looked much better than it felt – certainly to Fred. Every time she swirled, the skirt swirled, too, even when the rest of her stopped. As it did so, Fred's legs felt as though sharp blades were slicing into them. A beautiful delicate hand movement would end up with his getting slapped in the face by a sleeve which was a mass of sequins with fur cuffs but which felt as though it were made of solid steel. Each sleeve weighed thirty-five pounds.

Take after take of this number was shot and again it was the first one that was used.

Of course, the public were never aware of the problem caused by Ginger's dress. Nor did they know that when Fred was supposed to hit Randolph Scott in the film, he did just that. The gentle dancer for whom movement was an art hadn't learned how to aim a punch without hitting his 'opponent'. When Fred took a swing at Randolph, he actually drew blood.

Which was almost what some of the critics did. The *New York Post* declared that *Follow The Fleet* did not 'come within hailing distance of the glamorous and shining *Top Hat*, even though it does confirm the endlessly amazing talent of Fred Astaire.'

The public were less condescending. The box-office take was as high as was now expected of an Astaire-Rogers film and few complaints were heard from the paying public. Berlin made another small fortune from his score.

As well they might, everyone seemed to be more than happy at RKO, too. Or were they? Suddenly there was talk of bitter disagreement between the studio and Fred. There were rumours that he was going to court and was likely to leave Pandro S. Berman and everyone else at what was colloquially known as Radio Pictures.

His original contract with RKO was hardly the sort of document that was boasted about by superstars of the Astaire bracket. In fact, it was still basically the same one he had signed after taking those first hesitant steps over to the RKO lot for *Flying Down to Rio* – $1,500 a week with options of additional weekly sums of $500 while actually making a film.

In Follow the Fleet, *with music and lyrics by Irving Berlin, Fred and Ginger stage a benefit to save a ship.*

Fred said he wanted more money and discussions were begun with the studio – at first amicably and with everyone saying there was plenty of room for talking. But a new lawyer entered the fray on the Astaire side and the fight became altogether more bitter. Neither Fred nor the studio took to the change of tactics kindly. RKO thought about teaching a lesson to the man they considered was getting too big for his dancing shoes. They considered simply sitting back without offering Fred any more work for the time being. That way, they reasoned, they wouldn't even be obliged to pay him an extra $500 a week.

The row burst open – and with it came the first public news that perhaps things were not so good between Fred and Ginger either. Fred had let slip that he didn't think it wise for him to go on making too many pictures with Ginger.

'Ginger and I have made several together and have done almost every variety of dance,' he said at the time. 'People will begin to wonder if we aren't doing the same thing all over again.'

It was his old fear, that the public would soon get tired of both of them and of the vehicles that still had people lining up for blocks outside the theatres.

RKO quickly announced that they had no dissatisfaction with either star – the fact that Ginger had been making the same sort of noises almost from the beginning would not be allowed to interfere with a convenient policy line. Fred, too, denied he had any difficulties on that count. It was one of those private things that he wasn't willing to talk about. More frankly, he admitted that he wanted at least six months off so that he could visit Adele and Charles at Lismore Castle. He desperately wanted to be with his sister again. They hadn't had one of their heart-to-hearts since long before she had lost her twins, and the old intense feeling for each other was as strong as ever. If he had to go from one new movie to yet another, there wouldn't be time for a reunion.

A statement issued in Fred's name declared: 'The studio has violated my contract on several counts.' There were reports that he had been offered $400,000 for each of eight new pictures, and was still turning the studio down. 'He is legally sulking,' said the RKO men.

But before long, everyone in the affair announced they were happy. RKO said they had a new deal with their unlikely problem boy, and out of deference for the privacy of Mr Astaire, didn't tell anyone how much it was worth – although the previously mooted figures were close to the final amount. What was stated was that Mr Astaire would not be required to make more than two pictures a year. Ginger came on to the scene again now with the rather obvious announcement that

A gal and a gob.

Fred was also a singer. The biggest hit to come out of Follow the Fleet *was "Let's Face the Music and Dance."*

she wouldn't be required to make more than two pictures a year with Fred. She was, however, going to do a total of four films a year, and the other two would be starring vehicles for her alone.

If it was an amicable settlement, Fred was a lot less friendly when he heard about *Esquire* magazine and a jewellery firm who were advertising in that sophisticated journal. The firm ran a picture of Fred which clearly gave the impression that Astaire wore their jewellery. It was captioned: 'As inspired by Fred Astaire in *Top Hat*.' But he didn't wear it. In fact, Fred said the advertisement 'humiliated him and exposed him to ridicule.'

He was angry – more angry than he had been in public for a long time, and he sued.

Adele, meanwhile, decided not to wait for Fred to cross the Atlantic. She went to America herself and so was able to visit Fred and Phyllis and see their new son.

Astaire won his case. He was awarded $25,000.

Fred wasn't thinking of just six months' holiday. At thirty-six he was wondering whether the best of his dancing days were behind him.

No one could venture that it had all hardly yet begun; that the real Fred Astaire, the man with the unique quality of dancing like a youth while always acting his age, had still to etch himself a permanent place in history. So he felt he had to plan for every eventuality.

'If I cease to act and dance,' he said in 1936, 'I'll continue to compose and write.' But that could never really be a viable alternative for Fred Astaire.

Nor were these the only reasons. He couldn't really understand his popularity on the screen.

Fred, who now had the full right of refusal, was persuaded once more to look to his true value. Ginger, who had no say whatever in the matter, simply turned up on the lot at the right time and went to work on the new picture. It was, she was told, going to be called *Never Gonna Dance*.

For all the seemingly inseparable bond that had existed between himself and Adele, Fred had always been a lot tougher with her than he was going to be with Ginger – and in her own way, Ginger was a lot more co-operative. When Fred said rehearse, Ginger rehearsed, until both of them were exhausted but satisfied. It was a props man who discovered, before most people gave it a thought, just how hard Ginger did rehearse. He was mopping up the floor after yet another repeated take of what was then the title number 'Never Gonna Dance' when he noticed it was covered with a film of what looked suspiciously like blood.

At the time, Fred was out changing his shirt yet again and Ginger was hobbling to a corner of the sound stage, clutching a very red foot. The props man didn't realise that she was still wearing her shoe, but the blood had soaked right through the sides and sole of the satin dancing slipper and it all looked like a solid red mass. Despite Ginger's injuries, Fred called for yet another take – and he was still not satisfied. When it was shot again all looked perfect – until Fred himself spoiled everything by tripping up. In the end, just one more take was called for and everyone seemed content.

The picture was eventually given a new title, *Swing Time*, but there was little that was new about the story. It was the usual Astaire–Rogers mixture, with Fred playing a gambler and Ginger the girl who takes a hundred minutes to fall as hard for him as he did for her in the opening reel. Again, the principal ingredient in what served as the plot – apart from the comic relief supplied by Eric Bloore, Victor Moore and Helen Broderick – was deception; Fred pretending this time, of all things, that he couldn't dance. Ginger was a dancing teacher – which explains why. As usual they danced to a completely new set of routines. The policy of never repeating a dance step was followed as closely in *Swing Time* as in all the other films. The plot could be vaguely – and

Swing Time (1936) was directed by George Stevens and featured music by Jerome Kern.

Here he does "I'd Rather Lead the Band."

The only time Fred ever appeared in blackface was in the number "Bojangles of Harlem," in Swing Time. *The routine was inspired by the great black tap dancer Bill "Bojangles" Robinson.*

often, not so vaguely – similar from one picture to the next; the dance routines never.

And just as the dances were different, so were the tunes. Jerome Kern was the composer on the set once more, and for *Swing Time*, he created two new classics – 'A Fine Romance' and 'The Way You Look Tonight', both of which reflected the strange moral code that Astaire insisted upon for his pictures.

People had already begun talking about the way Astaire and Rogers conducted their film love affairs. No one minded that they were never seen in bed together, but they didn't even kiss. Absolutely never.

In 'A Fine Romance', lyricist Dorothy Fields emphasises it is a love affair 'with no clinches'. They don't kiss, so the story in the movie goes, because Fred is still engaged to the girl next door. In fact, he would have been married to her already had he not bothered so much about the turn-ups on his trousers that he made himself too late for the wedding.

Ginger has always said they never kissed on screen because she thought Fred was frightened Phyllis might get the wrong idea. As for himself, he has maintained he simply tried to avoid the 'mushy love scenes' adopted in every other film.

The treatment of 'The Way You Look Tonight' was another attempt at avoiding embarrassment. While the script called for Fred to sing to Ginger as she washed her hair in the bath, he was safe behind a locked door all the time. And just in case someone, somewhere, still got the wrong idea, Ginger was covered by a sea of opaque bubbles.

There was one other particularly notable number in *Swing Time*. For 'Bojangles of Harlem' and for the first and only time in his career, Fred worked in blackface, in a number inspired by Bill 'Bojangles' Robinson.

Kern worked hard on his numbers for the film, punching out tunes that sounded like magic from the keyboard of a proficient musician, but which from him resembled a collection of cowbells rung on an off day. It was Kern who kept a bust of Wagner staring down at him from the top of his piano – and who turned the head away when he felt he was disappointing the 'master'.

As for Fred and Ginger, there were rumours that they were about to disappoint the public. Ginger, it was reported, was getting more and more difficult to work with. She had banned visitors from the set while filming was going on. There was a sense of unease which was not helped by the constant change of title for the picture. *Never Gonna Dance* had become *Swing Time* and was then going to be called *Stepping Toes*; finally, and to most people's relief, it became *Swing Time* once more and stayed that way.

Was the Astaire–Rogers partnership going to last or had it really bitten the dust, never to recover again? Did the new contract make no difference, after all? Even Pandro Berman was forced to make a statement: 'I realise,' he said, 'that very soon I've got to face the certainty of breaking up my team.'

The talk now was that Fred and Ginger were both so determined to sever the partnership that RKO had to find ways and means of hinting at the inevitability of its happening sooner rather than later, if as painlessly as possible. The studio even revealed that Fred's next partner would not be Ginger, but Harriet Hoctor, who had appeared in *The Great Ziegfeld* and was about to go into the next stage production of the Ziegfeld Follies. But this turned out to be a kite that need never have been flown. Berman realised that Ginger was still safely in the bag for at least one more film. There were some critics, however, who were not sure whether that was a good or a bad thing.

For the first time there was less than unanimous approval for an Astaire–Rogers film.

RKO, for their part, wanted no more doubts. The next Astaire film would be with Ginger Rogers and that was all there was to it. The press, however, were not so easily convinced. Ginger's unhappiness with her fate as an also-ran to Astaire was not easily hidden. The two 'starring' vehicles that she was promised for her appearances without Fred were not even sops to her disappointment. Every one looked like it would be forgotten the moment 'The End' had flashed onto the screen. The rumors of dissent in the ranks were out in the open again. So RKO decided it had to dispatch emissaries to deny the very idea.

As for Fred, before anything else, he was going to take his holiday and this one was going to prove profitable. On his way to England with Phyllis, he stopped off in New York and did six fifteen-minute radio shows – at $4,000 a piece.

Everything he did on this English trip he did in a hurry – whether it was buying a couple of new suits, a dozen ties or giving an interview to C. A. Lejeune, the celebrated critic of *The Observer*. He talked to her in just three-and-a-half minutes flat. Miss Lejeune, who was one of the most respected film specialists in Fleet Street, had been waiting for that interview for more than two years. She had kept watch on the sailing lists week by week in the hope of finally catching up with Astaire. Eventually, she spotted his name and discovered that he would be staying at Claridges. On the day they met, she found him in the hotel lobby as he was about to rush through a side door, his coat-tails flying.

He was restless, she discovered, but 'charming and courteous, too'. He could not understand why people were interested in mobbing him, he told her. 'That sort of thing's silly and embarrassing. I've been in shows since I was seven. They could always see me. I've not changed.'

Was he limbering up for a new film? No. Work was always a matter of 'practice and thinking about ideas'. But he didn't like practising in public – because it was like reading a book with someone looking over your shoulder.

'I can't sing,' he told her. 'So why should I worry? It's all part of the routine and a new routine is the only thing that matters. I'm no better than I was when I was seven. Only more people see me.'

By 1937, Astaire and Rogers had already made half a dozen films together, and novel routines were getting harder to come by. In Shall We Dance, *dance director Hermes Pan put them on roller skates.*

The strange thing is that Astaire was about to experience the biggest single audience of his entire career – and almost nobody would see him at all. He was having another go at radio.

This development had begun at the tail end of Fred's holiday. He and Phyllis had gone over to Paris and were enjoying themselves immensely – mostly because they were able to keep out of the gaze of over-enthusiastic fans and newspaper men. But Johnny Green, who had conducted the orchestra for Fred on his records of film tunes on the Brunswick label, managed to reach him.

Green had been working with Jack Benny on the Jello program, which was beamed from New York through the Young and Rubicam advertising agency. The firm was now anxious to land Fred Astaire for their Packard motors show. Green, a dashing young man who never had any doubts about his own abilities, said he could achieve what Young and Rubicam had hitherto failed to pull off: contact Fred Astaire.

Over lunch, Green told Fred about the Young and Rubicam offer, and then handed him a piece of paper. It was a contract giving Green the option to play on the program if Fred accepted. Fred did accept and signed.

Again, he was going to have to dance on a small floor in front of two microphones and because, as he has said, he 'likes to cover ground' that was going to be as limiting to him as any one of the other problems faced by a dancer in sound broadcasting. To complicate matters still further, he and Ginger were about to start yet another new film, *Shall We Dance*.

A feature of the series was Astaire singing and reciting in dialect – 'I Love Louisa' in German, 'Christopher Columbus' in Italian and a couple of numbers featuring Englishmen and Scots thrown in for good measure. Green has described him as 'like a sophomore playing his first part in a high school dramatic play'.

One writer described Astaire's mastery of these antics as 'charming and insouciant', but at the end of the thirty-nine-week series, Fred called a halt. He had had enough. Phyllis preferred him knocking his brains out working on the routines for his films – if he had to work at all. She hoped that before long he would be able to give up show business and lead a more gentlemanly existence, but if he did have to work, the films were much more rewarding than standing in front of a microphone.

Radio was, however, *the* medium of the day. People who couldn't afford the price of even a suburban cinema ticket, could gather round a battered old radio set in their homes. But he had made his decision, and, although he would occasionally regret not carrying on with the work, he never again had his own regular radio series. One of the problems was that all the time he was rehearsing and broadcasting on

Shall We Dance. *The title says it all.*

the Packard Hour he was having to add on to the day already cut out for him on the set of *Shall We Dance* – which again had Pandro Berman producing and Mark Sandrich, who by now had established for himself almost a divine right to sit by the camera on an Astaire–Rogers set, directing.

The big songwriting team this time were the Gershwins. It seemed to be an unwritten law that the music on these films had to come from one of the big four – Porter, Berlin, Kern, or George Gershwin (with his brother Ira writing the lyrics).

For *Shall We Dance*, three out of the six Gershwin numbers became standards, 'They All Laughed', 'Let's Call The Whole Thing Off' and 'They Can't Take That Away From Me'. Of the other three, 'Slap That Bass' and '(I've Got) Beginner's Luck' were better than most of the songs heard in films of that time, and only the title song ever sounded less than strong. The story was, as usual, as weak as Hollywood tea. But that mattered no more now than it ever did. Fred this time was a ballet dancer who strangely enough looked just as good in top hat, white tie and tails as he did in a leotard.

The sensation in the film – and there always had to be one of those – was the sight of Fred and Ginger dancing on roller skates. They did this to the tune of 'Let's Call The Whole Thing Off' and the whole production number took an estimated thirty-two hours in preparation and four days in shooting. The pair covered approximately eighty miles in the process. The finished number lasted precisely two minutes forty seconds on the screen.

The roller skating trip through Central Park was Hermes Pan's idea. The notion of Astaire doing a dance in the engine room of a ship came from Pan, too – after noticing how Fred danced instinctively to the rhythm of a cement mixer they passed together on the street near the studio.

Shall We Dance itself was performed by the chorus, all wearing masks of lifesize photographs of Ginger's face.

There was one other important dance routine that Fred had in the picture – but it wasn't with Ginger. RKO had decided to bring Harriet Hoctor into *Shall We Dance* after all, even though she wouldn't be taking Ginger's place. In the picture's finale number, 'They Can't Take That Away From Me', it is Hoctor not Rogers, with whom Astaire is dancing.

It was, however, all Fred's and Ginger's picture. Ginger told *Picturegoer* magazine in October 1936: 'Having Fred as a partner and Hermes Pan for dance director has been a tremendous help to me. I know that I was better when dancing with Fred than I have ever been by myself. So he must get the credit. Fortunately, however, my style of dancing fits in perfectly with his. It's a sort of feminine Fred Astaire style, if you know what I mean.'

The way had been paved by the rumours, the counter-rumours and the leaks. But when the decision was finally announced that Ginger Rogers would not be in the next Astaire movie, it was still a shock to their fans.

The film was going to be an adaptation of the P. G. Wodehouse story, *A Damsel In Distress* and would be set in contemporary England, but filmed, of course, on the RKO lot. The man who wrote Jeeves had a story that the studio wanted to handle but RKO decided to put its own scriptwriters on to the job. When finally, even Pandro S. Berman agreed that their screenplay bore little resemblance to the Wodehouse story, he asked the expatriot Briton to have a go himself.

To an Anglophile like Fred the tale set in a quaint stately home seemed to be perfect. But with the certainty that Ginger wouldn't be in it, who could possibly take her place? It was a question much more easily asked than answered.

As the names were tossed about like press cuttings in a Hollywood office, stories about the possible rift between Fred and Ginger reached a crescendo. There could only be one reason that the pair had split up, the gossips decided. They hated the sight of each other and couldn't bear to be in one another's company. Matters were hardly helped by the intervention of Ginger's mother. Mrs Leila Rogers told pressmen, 'Ginger never had anything against Fred, nor has he against her. But she will be glad to get away from the team. Ginger is not only a dancer, but a screen personality and an actress.'

Fred said he was sure that the next film after *Damsel In Distress* would be with Ginger but it was getting harder and harder to find new stories. 'The more our films succeed, the more we have to live up to, and it seems the longer we have to wait till the right story comes along,' he declared.

The stories seemed to die down after that – particularly with the announcement that, really, Fred would have no new partner in *Damsel*. Instead, he would have most of the dance routines entirely to himself. He would, however, have a co-star – but she wouldn't do any dancing at all, apart from an occasional stroll with Fred.

And she wouldn't be English either. But the aristocratic Joan Fontaine seemed to measure up to most people's requirements at RKO.

There were the usual misunderstandings and traumas in the film. Fred was an American dancer who helps Lady Alyce Marshmorton (Joan Fontaine) escape from a fate worse than death.

There was also George and Ira Gershwin. They provided two classics for a film which, in retrospect, really didn't deserve them – 'Nice Work If You Can Get It' and 'A Foggy Day', the latter sung by Fred in full evening dress, sitting on a farm gate and contemplating life as the mist swirls around him.

But what about the comedy, that ingredient which Mark Sandrich had said was so well supplied by Fred and Ginger themselves when they were together?

Here, Pandro Berman had a stroke of genius. He borrowed George Burns and Gracie Allen from Paramount. The zany vaudeville act of Burns and Allen was one of the great joys of American entertainment of the period. On radio, George would ask Gracie why she insisted on putting salt in the pepper pot and she would reply: 'Everyone takes the salt when what they really want is the pepper. This time when they take the wrong one, they'll be right!'

The idea was that George would play Fred's press agent and Gracie, his secretary. Berman rightly believed it would be great casting. So did George Stevens, the director. It was up to Fred to decide as he had the final right of approving the cast – and particularly who was to dance in the pictures. There were plans for comedy dance routines with Burns and Allen. This worried George and Gracie, who were getting $10,000 a week for six weeks work – if Fred gave the scheme his stamp of approval. With Gracie, there were few problems. She came from a long line of Irish dancers and felt sure she could cope with anything Astaire wanted, particularly since he didn't have her in mind to replace Ginger.

The trouble was George, who seemed to be nothing more than one of the funniest men who ever trod a stage; who even pointed his cigar with great wit. But dance? As he says himself, he was a 'right-footed dancer'. He could hop a bit with his right foot, but his left foot had to be seen to be believed and after giving up his vaudeville dancing act, he preferred not to let anyone see it.

Eventually, he remembered a team of two vaudeville dancers with whom he and Gracie had played on the same bill a couple of times. They had a routine with a pair of whiskbrooms – brushing each other off in syncopation, with the brooms in effect becoming additional legs. Burns invited the surviving member of the duo to come and stay with Gracie and himself so that they could be taught the routine. The man stayed and got $500 for his trouble. It was $500 well spent.

Burns asked Fred if he would like to see a new dance he had devised. Fred said yes, he would – and he loved it. The whiskbrooms would be ideal for the film.

Was starring Fred in a film without a partner a good idea? The man for whom a team sounded like a pair of horses was never again to try going it quite so alone in a musical.

'The missing link between a smash Astaire hit and just good film fun,' said the *New York Journal,* 'is Ginger Rogers.'

It was a situation that couldn't last. Both Fred and Ginger – not to say Pan Berman and the other executives at RKO – realised that to make money, the team had to stick together. With that thought in mind, the studio announced that the next Astaire picture would be Astaire–

After Shall We Dance, *the Astaire-Rogers partnership was beginning to show some signs of strain.* Damsel in Distress *teamed Fred with Joan Fontaine.*

Among the supporting cast of Damsel in Distress *was the immensely popular comedy team of George Burns and Gracie Allen.*

In Carefree, *Fred and Ginger were back together again. "Fred Astaire and Ginger Rogers" had become a household word, and a diffi-cult habit for millions of movie fans to break.*

Rogers again. The title would be *Carefree* – which, as anyone who knew Fred could testify, was hardly an appropriate description of his attitude to life.

Carefree enabled Fred at last to combine business with pleasure.

In the film, Fred did a golf routine that is now remembered as nostalgically as the shooting of the men in *Top Hat* and the dancing of 'The Continental' in *Gay Divorcee*. While an off-screen orchestra played 'Since They Turned Loch Lomond Into Swing', Fred swung his golf-clubs with the precision of a surgeon doing open-heart surgery. It wasn't a dance in the conventional sense, but Fred made the clubs and balls swing rhythmically at his command. As usual, it was the result of dozens of takes over a period of two weeks – and was achieved only by the loss of over six hundred golf balls.

Part of the success of the number was due to the composer of the score, Irving Berlin, the only writer whose name habitually appeared on film credits in type either as big or even bigger than that used for the stars.

Carefree was not vintage Berlin, but the little man who only played his upright piano on the black notes, produced some pleasant enough numbers. One of the best was 'I Used To Be Color Blind' which, in typical Berlin style, was written to Doctor Astaire's prescription. No other songwriter has ever been able to provide songs that so perfectly match the requirements of a certain artist. Berlin made a profession of doing just that – right from the time he wrote Al Jolson's crie-de-coeur 'Let Me Sing And I'm Happy'.

He wrote 'I Used To Be Color Blind' because he was told *Carefree* was going to be the first Astaire–Rogers production in color. But the disappointing income from *Damsel In Distress* – it hardly came near the Astaire–Rogers productions – made Pan Berman and the men who controlled RKO's finances think again. It was one reason for Fred deciding that, before long, not only should he and Ginger part permanently, but he and RKO should go separate ways, too.

Carefree was, however, a *very* notable production. For in this film, at last Fred and Ginger actually do get to kiss – and seemingly for a very long time.

All sorts of new rumors had gone round as to why the two stars never did do that huddle. Ginger's feelings of embarrassment at possibly upsetting Phyllis had become magnified into tales of Mrs Astaire positively insisting that her husband should never kiss another woman. Fred constantly denied they were true. So for *Carefree* he decided to end the speculation for good – especially since a fan magazine had headlined a story 'Why Won't Fred Kiss Ginger?' And added four question marks to emphasise the importance of the query.

The historic clinch came at the end of the 'Color Blind' number.

The dance was done in slow motion and the kiss with it, with an additional few seconds ordered by the director Mark Sandrich – who was back in what many considered to be his rightful position – so that the scene could dissolve comfortably.

When the rushes of this historic number were ready, Phyllis decided that it was one moment when she ought to remember her responsibilities as a wife. She went along to the studio with Fred, which in itself was cause for speculation. At the end of the viewing session Phyllis looked at her husband – and said she noticed just how much he seemed to have enjoyed the experience.

Audiences especially relished it. People could be heard actually saying as they left the theatre, 'Fred's finally kissed Ginger.'

If the women were particularly captivated at the idea, the men could rejoice that Ginger never looked more beautiful. Since in *Carefree* she actually falls in love with Fred before he is smitten with her, the brittle front she adopted in the other films is softened as much as were the skin tones captured by the camera.

Berlin's one real hit tune of the film, 'Change Partners', seemed to have a symbolic ring about it after all the rumours of a split between the two stars – although the impact was reduced by the fact that *Carefree* did represent something of a reunion. 'Change Partners' stood on its own simply as a good song, which was more than could be said for most of the other numbers in the picture.

Carefree had no rapturous reception from critics or audiences. But it took money at the box office and the men at RKO were quick to talk about there being yet another Astaire–Rogers vehicle soon.

Astaire's was a voice to listen to. In September 1938, for the first time, he was listed in *Who's Who In America*. He was also stated to be one of America's richest men – *the* richest was William Randolph Hearst, whose year's salary checks had been worth $500,000. Fred came fifth in the list of best-paid actors – trailing Mae West, Bing Crosby, Charlie Chaplin and Will Rogers – after earning $127,875 in 1935, the year for which figures were now available. The money didn't necessarily impress Fred's fans, who were now constantly bombarding him with requests for old top hats, dancing shoes or anything he no longer had use for.

It was estimated that 70,000 people wrote to him every month.

Fred himself was always amused by these requests. But what interested him was the future, and apart from the dressing gown which still gave yeoman service at every preview of an Astaire film, there was little thought for souvenirs in his attitude. As he was to go on saying, he didn't like living in the past.

However, he would have been forgiven if perhaps, just once, he might have dreamed of going back to that past. *Time* magazine, without any warning, came out with the unbelievable statement that Fred Astaire was 'box office poison' and printed his photograph alongside their story as if to underline the fact. If that was Fred Astaire's 'present', then his 'past' seemed altogether more attractive.

The magazine picked up a list of stars which a major American theatre owner had published in a paid advertisement in one of the Hollywood trade journals. The strange thing was that Astaire's name was not on the original listings, although *Time* – for reasons that have never been properly explained – chose to add his name to all the others.

RKO called in their lawyers and were about to demand an apology when they decided to let the whole thing simmer down. Few people whose business was selling seats to Fred Astaire films thought he was anything like poison. Give them an Astaire–Rogers film every week, and the box office would look after itself.

Everyone now knew that wouldn't happen. Finally and with no punches pulled, RKO made the big announcement: The next Astaire–Rogers film will be the last.

With one of America's most prolific songwriters (over 3,000 songs), Irving Berlin.

Nobody really expected it would ever happen. There had been too many false alarms in the past. Surely, this was just an example of how a 'final retirement' would be followed by another still 'more final retirement' a year later?

There *was* more to it this time. The Astaire–Rogers films were still making money, but the pair were not succeeding in making every step they took seem as brand-new as it really was. It was not exactly a tired look, much more a growing suspicion that audiences were asking: 'So what are you going to do to impress us next?'

What they were, in fact, going to do as a final burst was to make a film about the couple who years before were such an influence on Fred and Adele – the Castles. Looking back, it seemed almost inevitable that Fred Astaire would one day feature in a film dedicated to Vernon and Irene Castle. In the days when he and his sister were just getting going in the big time, it was the Castles who were constantly being held up to them as the couple to follow. At one time, it seemed that *Variety* would bring the Castles' name into every piece they published on the Astaires.

Now, in 1938, if one looked for a couple who were closest to the Castles in contemporary terms, it could only be Astaire and Rogers. But that very factor presented a whole host of problems. For one thing, there could be no single composer brought in at ridiculous expense to write a complete score for the picture – as there had been for all but two of the films Fred had ever made.

The music in *The Story of Vernon and Irene Castle*, just had to be old – melodies to which the Castles themselves had danced all those years before. There would be a veritable feast of hotted up nostalgia, ranging from 'Oh You Beautiful Doll' through 'Waiting For The Robert E Lee' right up to 'It's a Long Way to Tipperary' and 'The Missouri Waltz' – this last tune played as Irene Castle 'dances' with the ghostly image of Vernon soon after he is killed in the Royal Flying Corps during World War One.

And that was the second difference between 'the Castles' – as invariably the film is now known – and the fluffy, near-plotless Astaire-Rogers films that had gone before it. No longer was there the silly young man who inevitably got his wires crossed trying to date the pretty but slightly aloof young lady. Gone, too, were the big white sets that made everyone wish he lived in a house that seemed to be a cross between a palace and an operating theatre; where never a speck of dust could be allowed to intrude, or a piece of furniture get out of place.

Now there was a true story, full of all the problems people in real life have to face and culminating in the biggest problem of all – death. Neither had ever played real characters in any of their joint films before and one of the weaknesses of the picture was probably a desperate attempt not to put a dancing foot wrong on or off the ballroom floor.

The picture's progress was anything but smooth, thanks to the rather formidable Mrs Irene Castle, now Mrs Irene McLaughlin, who had been retained as technical adviser on the picture.

81

In The Story of Vernon and Irene Castle, *Fred and Ginger portray the husband-and-wife dance team that had overwhelmed audiences twenty years earlier and lent their names to a new dance, the "Castle Walk."*

Even in her young days, Irene Castle was known as 'hell on wheels' and the now matronly Irene McLaughlin was doing little more than keeping up her old reputation.

The problems with Mrs McLaughlin came to a sudden end, thanks to a brilliant idea cooked up in Pandro Berman's office. It was the year California was debating whether or not to end vivisection a – subject about which Irene was known to care even more passionately than the dresses worn by Ginger Rogers. A secretary in Berman's office casually brought to her attention the news of a referendum on vivisection, with the sound advice that her views on the matter could sway the state's decision on the matter one way or another. The former ballroom queen was duly impressed and took off for the hustings immediately; leaving the entire production crew of *The Story Of Vernon and Irene Castle* to breathe very pronounced sighs of relief.

The reaction of the press was highly predictable, with almost every writer commenting on the change in the joint Astaire–Rogers appearance. It may have been too late to matter, but they really did still seem like a single person – or, at the very least like a pair of inseparable Siamese twins.

The *New York Times* commented: 'Rogers and Astaire have been so closely identified with light comedy in the past that finding them otherwise employed is practically as disconcerting as it would be if Walt Disney were to throw Mickey Mouse to the lions and let Minnie be devoured by a non-regurgitative giant.'

As if to apologise for its 'box office poison' slur, *Time* magazine let it be known they were laying out a red carpet for Astaire–Rogers and their new look.

'To say that Fred Astaire and Ginger Rogers are well fitted to fill the Castles' dancing slippers is an understatement,' the magazine commented. 'Astaire and Rogers symbolise their era just as completely as the Castles symbolised theirs.'

Fred and Ginger were still saying that they would make more pictures together – even if the RKO studio was more quiet than usual on the subject. But to show that both were still crazy about each other, the studio invited the press to meet them and get a few ideas about modern dancing.

The strains between them proved too great, and The Story of Vernon and Irene Castle *was to be Fred and Ginger's last picture together for nearly a decade. Here they are with Edna Mae Oliver and Walter Brennan.*

SOMETHING'S GOTTA GIVE

The end of the twilight was approaching. Chamberlain had come back from Munich waving his piece of paper and when Fred and Phyllis paid their last pre-war visit to England in May 1939, the euphoria of 'peace in our time' was beginning to wear off.

People still kidded themselves that there wouldn't be another major conflict and besides having a vacation, this was Fred Astaire's way of showing he had faith in human nature.

As the liner *Georgic* docked at Cork – Fred was introducing Phyllis to Ireland and making a stay at Adele's castle the first part of their itinerary – he said: 'We have chosen a European holiday because we like Europe and we don't believe that the folk here are so silly as to go to war.' Then, wearing a bright yellow scarf, and with Phyllis in a fur coat, they drove off with Lord Charles Cavendish in the direction of Lismore.

It was in Fred's and Phyllis's judgement their first real holiday in five years – and the first without a contract with RKO. As he and Ginger finished *The Castles*, he had also finally severed his links with the outfit which had given him international fame.

What would he do when the vacation was over? MGM had signed him to make *Broadway Melody of 1939* and for some three years there had been talk of starring Fred in another biographical picture – this time as Nijinsky. Phyllis approved of that one – probably because she thought that it gave some proper recognition of his true dancing worth. But Fred was not so sure. 'It would take me three years of rehearsals before I could approach him.' The idea, he said, 'scared me stiff.'

He didn't consider himself a new Nijinsky either, simply a hoofer who enjoyed doing what he did for a living more than anything else. Now, on holiday, he was trying to spend all his time racing, fishing and playing golf. He did venture, however, that he missed being with Fred Junior and Peter, Phyllis's elder son, who was now away much of the time at boarding school.

'There's no secret about married happiness,' he declared. 'It's fate. We are the happiest couple in the world.' In the words of the press handouts that bombarded every show business writer's desk on both sides of the Atlantic, 'we're made for each other.'

Meanwhile, he was also delighted to be back once more with Adele – 'She's definitely retired. And she looks as well and happy as I've ever seen her.'

They seemed to be talking every night away with memories of the past and their thoughts on the present and future.

When the holiday finally came to a halt, Fred had to settle down to *Broadway Melody of 1939*, which was so long being discussed that it had now become *Broadway Melody of 1940*. There had been ten of these annual tributes to the street that was the real cradle of transatlantic showbiz and, although no one knew it at the time, this was going to be the last.

Broadway Melody of 1940 *teamed Fred with not one, but two partners, Eleanor Powell and George Murphy. Music and lyrics by Cole Porter.*

Fred danced his way through
Second Chorus *with*
Paulette Goddard, who had
come to Hollywood as
Charlie Chaplin's protégée.
The film was a flop.

But who would dance opposite Fred in this magnum opus? There were no doubts whatever that it wouldn't be Ginger. But who else was there? It was MGM who finally resolved the question. They would co-star Fred – but *not* 'team' him, it was stressed – with probably the finest girl dancer of the age, Eleanor Powell. When the news of the possible partnership first broke, newspaper columnists wondered if two already established stars like Astaire and Powell could possibly work together – particularly on the terms Fred invariably imposed.

Fred, who always kept abreast of the market, greatly admired Miss Powell. He conceded that she 'danced like a man' – by which he didn't mean that she had lost any of her femininity; simply that she had the same sort of stamina and, more important, discipline that he expected of himself. But he *was* worried about her as a partner, and it was the same worry that constantly cropped up whenever a new dancer's name was considered in the context of facing him on a stage or a film set: was she too tall?

Fred, as it happened, measured 5 ft 9¾ inches and Eleanor was two-and-a-quarter inches shorter. But he couldn't be sure and he let his doubts be known to the MGM bosses.

It was Louis B. Mayer himself who suggested to Eleanor that she should make the film, but even he was worried about the height problem. It called, he decided, for a confrontation – and the scenario he adopted could have fitted beautifully into any matrimonial comedy of the period being made by his studio; he suggested that she come to his room at the same time that Fred was there – but without letting him know. While Mayer and Astaire were talking, he said, Miss Powell would be hiding behind the large wood-panelled office door.

That was precisely what happened – although, unlike a film story –

she didn't hear anything she shouldn't. The conversation was extremely complimentary to the lady. Finally, the mogul put Eleanor out of her misery and revealed to Fred that she had been with them all the time – and wouldn't it be a good idea if, once and for all, they stood back to back with each other? They did – and everything looked just fine. But with Fred what 'looked' fine was not always good enough. He had to see how they danced together before he committed himself. In the rehearsal room at the studio, specially fitted for him with long mirrors, Astaire pronounced himself content.

Mirrors played an important part in the picture itself. For the 'Begin the Beguine' number, which alone would have made this *Broadway Melody* a notable film, Fred and Eleanor danced before a sixty foot mirror that had been fixed by the engineers to a moving track. As it rotated, the mirrors had the effect of changing the backgrounds for the routine.

There was not much to be said about the story of *Broadway Melody* – no more, in fact, than there had ever been for an Astaire–Rogers picture. It was about putting on a big Broadway show, with Fred as the hard-working dancer who achieves a well-deserved success near the end of the picture. If it all seemed vaguely reminiscent of *Dancing Lady*, perhaps no one ought to have been surprised. It was in that picture at MGM that Fred had made his debut. Now, as the studio said, he was home again.

George Murphy, a song and dance man who went on to become a United States senator, was one of the other stars in the film and there were a few delightful moments too, from Frank Morgan, fresh from the title role in *The Wizard of Oz*.

But it was Astaire and Powell who made the picture – with generous help from Porter's music. One of the numbers he wrote especially for the film was the celebrated 'I Concentrate On You'. Another was 'I've Got My Eyes On You'. Which was precisely what the critics had on Astaire and Powell, wondering whether there would ever be another joint venture. As it turned out, there never would be – but the studios could have done a lot worse.

The film arrived in the theatres soon after Fred's optimism about the world situation was finally shattered. Europe had been 'silly enough' after all, to get embroiled in a new war. To an Anglophile like Fred, sitting at home in Beverly Hills made him feel almost isolated. Adele was still in Ireland and Astaire knew they were unlikely to see her this side of the peace settlement, whichever way that went and in 1940 no one could be sure which way that would be.

During those early days of the war, Fred kept in close touch with all his English friends. Letters went in both directions across the Atlantic, between Fred and Delly; Fred and David Niven and Fred and George Griffin, who had at one time been his valet in London.

Delly was not quite alone in war-time Britain. She not only had Lord Charles, who was an Army officer, but her mother was with her too. Fred sent Mrs Astaire Senior, parcels of Californian dried fruit.

'Delly' wrote to him on their mother's behalf. 'It is marvellous. Food is going to be scarce here, so it's grand to have such luxuries.'

In the States, luxuries came in more costly packages. One of these was a Fred Astaire film that might have benefited all concerned if it had been part of an economy drive and just never allowed to happen.

Second Chorus marked Astaire's entry into Paramount Studios. It came at a time when Hollywood considered its main task to be making a declaration of normality. Fred was desperately worried about England. His friend David Niven and a few of the other members of the film town's English colony may have decided their duty was to go home, but for almost everyone else in Hollywood, Europe was a long way off. Normality was escape and *Second Chorus* should have been allowed to escape without trace – but it didn't.

It was a symptom of the disease that doctors might have called Gingervitis – had they not already used a similar word for an entirely different malady.

With Ginger as a 'natural' opposite Fred, and with Eleanor Powell unavailable for more films in the forseeable future, studios seemed to develop a mental blockage when it came to completing an Astaire cast list. They refused to accept that he could more than adequately hold a dancing picture on his own and insisted, instead, on giving him a starring partner. For *Second Chorus*, Paramount chose a beautiful, dark-haired girl who could be a stunning actress; she and her husband also lived near Fred's Beverly Hills home on Summit Drive. The girl was Paulette Goddard, fresh from the triumph with her husband Charles Chaplin in *The Great Dictator*, she was not known as a dancer and *Second Chorus* hardly provided her with that additional qualification. Yet dance she did in this film – if to no one's great pleasure.

Hermes Pan did his best with her and Paulette's long legs clad in the sheerest black tights that those pre-nylon days could offer, were enticing. But she never looked like a professional dancer. The studio – as seemingly did all studios – insisted on a name to bring in the customers, while Pan would dearly have preferred an opportunity to take in an unknown who simply danced well.

Like most of the films, it represented something like six to seven months work. It could have taken much longer, and not simply because of the problem of making Miss Goddard into a dancer. Paramount executives were reported at the time to wake up in the middle of the night in cold sweats—not knowing whether the writers of the piece would ever finish the story. When it was all finally and safely locked in the can, you could almost hear the sighs of relief around Hollywood.

No one doubted that Fred and Paulette Goddard had made their first and last picture together. Early in 1941, the name of a new partner was announced. She was only twenty-two but she had a name that evoked memories of Fred's days in vaudeville.

Fred Astaire could not possibly have known that the day he signed a contract with Columbia Pictures he was helping to write a chapter in the history of the cinema.

On the surface, going to Columbia was an odd thing to do. True, it was an outfit that occasionally had its moments of glory – the Frank Capra films were an example – but no one considered it any more a prestige studio now than they had when Gable was unceremoniously unloaded there.

Astaire, however, was more concerned with finished products than with the prestige of the people for whom he worked. Had he not been, he would never have stayed so long with RKO, which at one time was even more poverty-stricken than Columbia.

He also had one distinct advantage over other players who crossed the studio threshold. His name.

Harry Cohn, the iron dictator of Columbia whose reputation made him a cross between Hitler and Judas, wouldn't dare drop cigar ash on Astaire the way he did on to almost everyone else. It is even possible he muted his usual vocabulary in Fred's presence. But Astaire didn't go to Columbia because he liked Cohn, or because he was attracted by the story idea they presented to him – although it did for once take note of the fact that other nations were at war and American kids were thinking about putting on uniforms. What interested him far more was a girl he had heard was under contract at Poverty Row.

She hadn't made much of an impact, even at Columbia. She had been making a Blondie picture or two and had also had odd parts in other B pictures. But he hadn't seen them. Nor had he met her. But it was her name that fascinated him – Margarita Cansino.

By the time Fred had signed his contract, the girl had been given a new name by Cohn.

The name he chose for her, he thought, was much more suitable, much more American. And it was only partly made-up, because he used her mother's maiden name. She became Rita Hayworth.

Fred had watched her work and liked what he saw. Now, Harry Cohn told her that she was to get her first starring role – and her new name would be perfect for it.

It was a very excited and very shy Rita Hayworth who took her first tentative steps alongside Fred on the Columbia lot for a picture to be called *You'll Never Get Rich*.

As the days went by, Rita became less shy and more sure of herself. But she says now she never stopped being excited at working with Fred Astaire, a 'real gentleman'. She also experienced the usual penalty of any Astaire co-star – hard work, Astaire style.

The starring debut of Rita Hayworth is now the only thing for which *You'll Never Get Rich* deserves to be remembered. It was a very slight story about a Broadway dancer who gets drafted. The locale of an Army rookie introduction centre was based on a real military camp, but Fred's uniform – he becomes an officer, of course – looks stagey

and no one really imagined you could ask Fred Astaire to peel potatoes while in training.

It should have been much more notable – for Cohn now decided to take another leaf out of RKO's book and hire not just any songwriter to do the picture score, but one of the Greats, Cole Porter.

The tunes – 'The Boogie Barcarolle'; 'Shootin' The Works For Uncle Sam', 'Since I Kissed My Baby Goodbye'; 'So Near And Yet So Far' and 'Wedding Cake Walk' – give some idea of the sort of material he provided for the movie. None was in the least bit memorable; in fact, it was the only time Porter wrote a score that failed to produce a single hit.

One of the problems at the time was that ASCAP – which still proudly boasted Fred Astaire as a fully paid-up member – had called a strike and none of the new tunes were getting radio airings. Rita wasn't happy with the way the music was handled in the film, either. Harry Cohn flatly refused to allow her to sing in the picture.

When Columbia decided on another Astaire-Hayworth picture to follow fairly soon afterwards, Fred greeted the idea with considerably more enthusiasm than he usually accepted a repeat performance. He was as determined as ever not to be part of a 'team' again, but there was something rather special about the red-headed Miss Hayworth, who in a sweater was now brightening up many a real Army barrack-room.

Before the new Hayworth film was underway, there were two other new productions for Fred to consider. The first starred Bing Crosby; the second Phyllis Astaire. They were on holiday when she told him that she was pregnant.

In 1941, a young newcomer to Hollywood—the daughter of Eduardo Cansino, whom Fred had known during his vaude-ville days—co-starred in You'll Never Get Rich*. A year later, her picture was to grace millions of GI lockers. Her name: Rita Hayworth.*

Ever since Ginger had given way to a host of other leading ladies, people had been asking Fred which one of them he liked best. He always shrugged the famous Astaire shoulders and changed the subject. Now, at last, he had a partner he could hold out as being head and shoulders above all the others – and for once the height just didn't matter.

In *Holiday Inn*, he was teamed with Bing Crosby – and from that moment on he had the pat answer to the inevitable question. His favourite partner was 'Bing'. Though he could have had reason to resent Mr Crosby.

For one thing, this was going to be the first Astaire film in which Fred didn't get the girl. For another, *Holiday Inn* produced the most sensational song hit of all time – 'White Christmas', which as everyone who has ever listened to a radio during the festive season knows, was Bing's hit, not Fred's.

By all accounts, Fred enjoyed *Holiday Inn* as much as any film he had ever made – and worked just as hard in it, shaping the routines as only a perfectionist could.

It was the story of a hotel owner who wanted to keep his place open just for the holidays. Bing was the owner of the Holiday Inn; Fred – the star dancing attraction who unsuccessfully tries to woo Marjorie Reynolds away from him.

Bing had most of the good songs – and 'White Christmas', which has now sold more than ninety million copies (twenty-five million of them Crosby's), was the best. Irving Berlin says of that one – 'It's quite impressive.' And that from a man who has had more hit songs than any other popular composer.

In fact, it was due to Berlin who was one of Fred's closest friends in all his years' hoofing, that *Holiday Inn* ever got on to the Paramount floor. He had long before dreamed up the idea of staging a musical show based on seasonal numbers. One of his greatest previous successes had been 'Easter Parade', and the number played more than any other on the Fourth of July was 'God Bless America' which at one time was considered likely to replace the 'Star Spangled Banner' as America's National Anthem.

The stage show never came about, but a meeting between Berlin and Mark Sandrich in New York clinched the idea of its forming a reasonable basis for a movie. Berlin wanted Crosby for the principal role and since Sandrich was now a top producer for Paramount, Bing's studio, it was a reasonable suggestion. Sandrich, for his part, thought it would be a superb idea to be able to team Mr Crosby with his old star Fred Astaire – who could, he reasoned, play Bing's ex-vaudeville partner.

It was not an easy plan to put before the bosses of Paramount. Crosby was expensive, but he was under contract, so that was fine. Astaire, on the other hand, was a free agent – and he came very costly. It was also war time and the whole nation was constantly being exhorted to economise. Fred Astaire and Bing Crosby in one picture looked very extravagant indeed.

Finally, a deal was settled – with the understanding that at least the leading lady would not be paid too much. In typical Hollywood fashion, there turned out in the end to be two leading ladies – Marjorie Reynolds whom Fred didn't get, and Virginia Dale whom he did. Neither had a particularly devastating effect on the pockets of the Paramount stockholders.

As a result of making *Holiday Inn*, no one had cause for complaint. Berlin, unloading a calendar full of seasonal melodies ranging from 'Let's Start The New Year Right' to 'White Christmas' – with 'Easter Parade' and tunes for Lincoln's birthday and the Fourth of July thrown in between – had cause to laugh hysterically all the way to the bank.

A couple of months before the film opened, Phyllis completed her own major production. Her third baby – the second with Fred – was a daughter. They called her Ava. There is said to be something very special about the relationships between fathers and daughters and, as the years went by, Fred and Ava were to more than prove the point.

The success of Fred's marriage to Phyllis had always been an open secret. They still avoided parties and big social gatherings, but that only went to show the film colony how happy and self-contained they were. At a time when comedians were making popular sport about Hollywood marriages – one tale was that brides were wished 'Many Happy Returns' on their wedding day – Fred and Phyllis were con-constantly refuting the legend.

Dancing his way through Holiday Inn, *with Marjorie Reynolds and Virginia Dale. The film co-starred Bing Crosby. The Claude Benyon–Elmer Rice screenplay featured music and lyrics by Irving Berlin.*

The title of Astaire's next picture, his second in 1942, seemed to be a paean to Phyllis: *You Were Never Lovelier*. It also made a strong impact on the cinema.

This was Fred's second, and as it turned out, last, vehicle with Rita Hayworth, who really never was lovelier than in this story of four Argentinian sisters. It was based on a film bought in the Argentine by the producer, Louis F. Edelman. The Latin-American locale was immensely suitable, bearing in mind Rita's own background. But the only thing to show the film was set in Buenos Aires was the orchestra of Xavier Cugat. The music of Jerome Kern and Johnny Mercer, however, was spectacularly Hollywood – and Hollywood at its best.

Fred sang 'Dearly Beloved' and 'You Were Never Lovelier' and Rita Hayworth, still unable to convince Columbia Pictures she should be allowed to do her own thing, mouthed 'I'm Old Fashioned' to the voice of Nan Wynn.

Kern made no bones about writing the sort of music with which he felt comfortable. Fred liked Xavier Cugat's style, but Kern refused to write anything specially for him. 'I don't write Spanish songs', he told Lou Edelman. 'I don't write anything unless I can write it well and I can't write Spanish songs.'

Rita didn't have enough dancing roles after *You Were Never Lovelier*, although the later *Cover Girl* was to be a big milestone in her career. She was going to be groomed now as a serious actress and, as she puts it, 'pushed further ahead to stardom'.

Time magazine said: '*You Were Never Lovelier* presents fresh evidence that Fred Astaire is still a superb dancer and a deft light comedian and that Rita Hayworth is still the most ambrosial lady he has ever teamed with.'

In 1942, Fred started thinking about a new kind of engagement. He called in to see his local draft board.

In March that year, soon after the birth of Ava, he appeared in a list of possible draftees, in the company of Jack Oakie, Spencer Tracy and Humphrey Bogart, but at the age of forty-two he was very low down in that list; he was, in fact, number 156. Yet he didn't want to either escape the hazards that many less favoured men were facing every day or even to be thought to be avoiding them.

For stars like Astaire, the Government had missions which, in their way, were as important as sitting with a gun in a foxhole – entertaining the troops and helping to raise money for the war effort.

Pearl Harbour had totally changed the outlook of most Americans, and just as the name of the base struck down by the Japanese Air Force in December 1941 had become engraved in history, so the words 'war bonds' had become part of many people's everyday vocabulary. They were sold the way soap and cigarettes had been sold in peacetime.

A Hollywood Bond Victory Cavalcade had been organised, taking stars on bond-selling trips from one end of America to another and Fred was one of the first to join this outfit.

It was like the old Orpheum vaudeville circuit again – going from one tank town to another, singing a song one minute, dancing a number the next, and then a few minutes later holding out his hands and asking the audience to buy a bond for America. Fred and the other Cavalcade members played at Service bases, in village halls, at celebrity banquets and in theatres, both big and small. An exhausting experience, but worth every minute spent on it and every dollar saved in war bonds.

At a rally in New York's Madison Square Garden, an Astaire performance helped take the city's bond sales past the goal of five billion dollars. A war bond was the only admission price to the rally, and there were 18,500 seats up for the asking – for upwards of $25 each. Half of the Garden seats were for buyers willing to spend a minimum of $100. Altogether, the boxes cost a staggering $2 million each to hire. That night alone brought in $86,000,000.

For Fred, making the bond drives was even harder than rehearsing for a Broadway show or a Hollywood film. In between Victory Cavalcade assignments, he was pressed by the studios to think of his conventional work. RKO still clung to the fond belief that they could persuade Fred to link with Ginger once more and said that they even had a new film prepared by David Hempstead ready to shoot. But it didn't happen quite like that.

Hempstead did entice Fred back to RKO. But the partner was not going to be Ginger. Instead, they had lined up an eighteen-year-old girl who had just had a taste of Hollywood stardom side by side with James Cagney in the picture *Yankee Doodle Dandy*, Joan Leslie.

The film was to be called *The Sky's The Limit* with music by Harold Arlen – four years earlier, he had had his triumph with 'Over The Rainbow' for Judy Garland – and lyrics by Johnny Mercer.

Before filming got under way, Irving Berlin returned to Hollywood from his New York home with an offer to star Fred in his forthcoming *Music Box Revue*. The Revue had been Berlin's answer in the twenties to the Ziegfeld Follies. But Fred was not ready to return to Broadway and Berlin was soon planning other things – notably the most successful military show of all time, *This Is The Army*.

Fred was by now letting his mind stray to retirement again. But first, he had to complete *The Sky's The Limit* and then do some more entertaining for the war effort. If he could also go overseas, so much the better.

The big hit tune of the new film was the one that has since become the national anthem of alcoholics the world over – 'One For My Baby'. Fred is reputed to have actually tanked himself up with at least one glass of something strong before filming of the number began – to get into the right, should we say, spirit. But it is safe to add that no one imagined it would have quite the impact on drinkers that it did.

Fred played a member of the Flying Tigers squadron in the picture and Joan Leslie, a magazine photographer. In the true spirit of the times, when Fred wasn't in uniform he wore a dinner jacket, not white tie and tails.

He also improvised a number on the spot. In one scene, Robert Ryan and Richard Davies were supposed to entice Joan away from Fred, but couldn't find a way to do it effectively.

'You've got to do something to him – something cruel,' Hempstead told them.

In the end, Fred dreamed up the idea of a snake dance to, supposedly, frighten away the opposition. He climbed up on a table and performed the dance, but instead of frightening anyone, Joan said it all reminded her of Dorothy Lamour.

Meanwhile, the idea of Fred playing a Flying Tiger who spent much of his time out of uniform provoked a few comments in the press. One critic wanted to know how a soldier could go around on leave in civilian dress. Other critics wanted to know what Fred Astaire was doing in a film like *The Sky's The Limit*. The *New York Times*'s Bosley Crowther was extremely disappointed with it all: 'Mr Astaire does one solo which is good, but a bit woe-begone, and the rest of the time he acts foolish – and rather looks it – in his quick-fitting clothes.'

Fred was equally unsure about his next professional assignment – but there was nothing new about that attitude. He always was unsure. He joined MGM for a part in the studio's revue spectacular *Ziegfeld Follies*, which also included stars like Fannie Brice, Esther Williams, Lucille Ball, Kathryn Grayson, Lena Horne and Red Skelton. William Powell played the part of a now dead Ziegfeld recalling the great days of the Follies from his heavenly perch. Astaire was the man he said he would choose to lead a contemporary Follies.

Fred himself had suggested one of his big numbers 'Limehouse Blues' to producer Arthur Freed. He did this spectacular with Lucille

In The Sky's the Limit *(1943), Fred plays a member of the Flying Tigers who goes on a spree in New York and meets magazine photographer Joan Leslie.*

Ziegfeld Follies (1946) was Fred's first color film, and featured an all-star cast that included Lucille Ball, Fannie Brice, Judy Garland, Red Skelton, Lena Horne, William Powell, and Gene Kelly. Sixteen years earlier, Fred and Adele had starred in the Ziegfeld show Smiles.

Bremer. The film also featured a revival of the nonsense number he had sung with Adele in *Funny Face* – the Gershwins' 'Babbit and the Bromide'. This time, he performed it with Gene Kelly.

Film revues don't usually succeed – but *Ziegfeld Follies* did. And one of the reasons it did was, without doubt, Fred Astaire.

As soon as his commitment to MGM was over, Fred put on a uniform – and for the first time, it was for real. He had enlisted in the USO, the organisation which liked to call itself Soldiers in Greasepaint. The bigger the star, the further away the USO were happy to send him – and as the tentacles of the advancing allied armies spread over enemy-occupied territory, so the field of operations of these entertainers extended. They wore officer's uniforms, but no badges of rank.

Fred was told he was going to London – which, as far as he was concerned, was just about the one place he wanted to be more than any other. It meant not only a reunion with the city that had been a second home, but also with Adele – who was barely over yet another tragedy in her life.

Early in March 1944, her husband, Lord Charles Cavendish had died. It was a lonely death. He had been ill for some time, and all that time, Adele was hundreds of miles away working in London for the American Red Cross. Her mother had been nursing him at Lismore during his last days because Adele couldn't get a permit to cross the Irish Sea. It was just before D-Day.

By the time Fred was ready to fly the Atlantic, Adele had got over the initial shock of Charlie's death and was back at work at Rainbow Corner – the social centre in London's Shaftesbury Avenue for the hordes of American Servicemen thronging the capital just before they sailed for Europe.

If people had previously had doubts about Adele's identity, the night that Fred joined her at the Corner, they were put aside. Fred was instantly recognisable and the people there reacted accordingly. With him was his own personal accordionist, Mike Olivieri who had just been half way round the world as a one-man orchestra, and there were a few members of Glenn Miller's celebrated outfit at the club, too. Miller himself had only just embarked on the fog-bound cross-Channel flight from which he never returned.

Entertaining the troops had become an honoured tradition in the United States. It was show business's effort for the country, and those who volunteered for work with the USO were simply doing their own kind of soldiering. Glenn Miller was not the only casualty 'Over There' – to quote the George M. Cohan tune that was virtually the USO's theme song.

When, after kissing Delly goodbye again, Fred boarded an aircraft at London's Northolt Airfield, he knew he could be the next to disappear. But he was consoled by the company he kept. With him on the cross-channel flight, the first leg of the trip to the front line, was

Bing Crosby. Bing was as disturbed as he was at having a pilot for the journey who looked no more than seventeen, but they all got over to France in one piece.

Fred and Bing enjoyed being with each other – but if anyone had thoughts of their reliving the experience of *Holiday Inn*, with Bing calling all the shots, there was no cause. For days, the Groaner bemoaned the fact that he was virtually unrecognised by the girls in the small French town where they awaited their next orders. On the other hand, there were swarms of nubile young ladies around Fred – after one of them found an ancient fan magazine which had printed his portrait. Everybody loved Fred Astaire – although he wasn't quite prepared for the welcome from one small boy who told him how pleased he was to meet Mr Ginger Rogers.

As impressed as the young troops were with Fred Astaire, he was more moved himself by what he saw in the places where he and Mike the accordianist entertained.

'They've unbelievable guts,' was all he could say after seeing one group of men return from action. 'They go back in there time and time again to hit the Germans. It's something impossible to forget.'

He danced wherever the authorities would let him go – and generally it was close enough to hear the guns bursting; frequently so close that he had to be advised to move back. Everywhere he went he carried a six by twelve foot mat, so that he could dance as near as possible in the style to which he had become accustomed. Often, he performed wearing heavy Army boots.

The boys, like soldiers anywhere had a one-track mind once they could forget the horror of the fighting. As much as they liked his dancing – and they were as impressed as anyone could be at having a live performance by Fred Astaire – the questions revealed what they were really thinking. In almost every place he and Mike stopped he was asked the same question: 'Say, what's it like to have a pretty girl like Rita Hayworth in your arms?'

Fred was nonchalant with his answer: 'Just fine,' he told them. 'She's a beautiful dancer.'

The head of the USO camp shows in Europe, Bill Dover, was suitably impressed with the Astaire performances. Word got back to him of Fred and the Chicago comedian Willie Shore being caught up in a German counter-attack near the front line in Belgium. It was just before the massive offensive that has become known in history as the Battle of the Bulge – the last, dangerous but finally futile attempt of the Germans to regain the initiative in the war.

Fred and the comedian were moving up towards their next show when the Luftwaffe decided to put on a show of its own spraying bullets and bombs around them like the firecrackers in the Fourth of July number from *Holiday Inn*. All Fred is prepared to admit today is that he landed up in a ditch for a little while. The stories circulating about the incident at the time said that he and Shore were pinned to the muddy ground, and under fire all the time, for twelve hours.

Dover, a Hollywood executive in peacetime, had himself just experienced the thrill of having a German bullet whizz past his nose. But it was the bravery of Fred Astaire he kept talking about.

'Funny thing about Astaire,' he said later. 'He was rather nervous about going under fire for a number of reasons – including his wife and the kids. But he was tremendous after that twelve-hour introduction to fire and it all went without a hitch.'

He entertained wherever there were people to listen to him. Sometimes he played to two hundred, sometimes, two thousand.

Fred made no distinction as to rank on this tour. When General Eisenhower asked to see him, Fred performed for the Allied Commander in Chief just as though he had been a buck private.

He did between three and four shows a day; sometimes to 'footloggers' waiting for the next order to advance; sometimes to airmen about to 'scramble' on a raid over enemy territory. If he were lucky, the camp entertainments officers made makeshift platforms for him but frequently he had to use the back of trucks for his dancing. If the mat had to serve as his entire stage, he'd make do with whatever he had around him. In Army hospitals he leapt from one empty bed to another. In barracks rooms he jumped on and off tables – using every gadget in the sparse room as a prop.

The real triumph in what must be regarded as his finest hour, came at the end – when in September 1944, he gave the first concert since the liberation in the famous Paris music hall, the Olympia. There were two thousand American troops in the audience. It was Fred's first appearance ever on a French stage.

Afterwards, it took all the strength that the Military police could muster to hold back the hundreds of eager French fans beseiging the theatre, waiting for Fred to leave the stage door. 'Vive Monsieur Astaire,' they shouted as they thrust autograph books in his direction.

Then he went back to the front – where on one occasion, he got so exuberant that his taps flew out into the audience. 'It's more dangerous on the front row with me dancing than it is on the front line,' he quipped.

Fred and Bing Crosby met up again for the journey back to the States, travelling in the *Queen Mary*, which had been converted to a troop ship at the start of the war. They gave a number of shows for the boys on board, including some for the wounded in the ship's hospital.

When he finally reached America, he spoke again of the Allied troops – 'Unbelievable guts'. The boys, he declared, 'left an indelible impression.'

Phyllis met him in New York. Before they left together for California, Fred spent days on the telephone – calling not just his own family, but making several hundred calls to wives, mothers and sweethearts of the Servicemen he had met overseas. Not all of the boys were coming back; but the messages Fred delivered were from young men who had had an experience they were not going to forget – and part of that unforgettable experience was meeting Fred Astaire.

In 1944, Fred went overseas to entertain troops. Adele, whose English husband died in March of that year, devoted herself to war relief work. Brother and sister were reunited after a separation of several years.

Doing a troop show in front of Versailles, outside of Paris.

Lucille Bremer (Yolanda) and Fred Astaire (the Thief).

Back home on Summit Drive, Fred was much more a happy husband and father than a returning hero. Peter and Fred Junior were given the captured Iron Crosses and other German insignia he brought with him, and if the younger Fred Astaire – now eight years old – had made it clear he wasn't going to be a hoofer like his dad, that was quite all right. Fred was just pleased to be back and Phyllis was glad to have him home.

All Fred wanted to do now was to relax and think very seriously about retirement. *Ziegfeld Follies* had not been shown yet and until it was, Astaire was his usual worrying self. But not even a hit would let him stray from the idea of resting.

He agreed to make one more picture at MGM and then the dancing shoes were going to be hung up for good. Doctors had told him that nobody approaching forty-six should consider taxing his heart the way Fred did every time he danced on a stage or film set.

No one who saw Fred's next picture, *Yolanda And The Thief* would have blamed him for turning to dramatic roles either. It was a fantasy played for much of the time against a backcloth that would have suited Snow White. It didn't really suit Fred Astaire or the box office. But it teamed Fred once more with Miss Lucille Bremer, who after her two parts with Astaire in *Ziegfeld Follies* and *Yolanda* decided to settle for marriage.

All the time that Fred was working on *Yolanda* people were asking the now expected questions: 'What next? Would he really pack it all in after so long?'

For a time it seemed he would not. MGM believed they still had a commitment from him for more pictures and they already had a new title they wanted him to make – an updated version of *Belle of New York*, a Broadway show stopper at the turn of the century.

As Fred rehearsed his numbers for *Yolanda*, songwriters Harry Warren and Johnny Mercer tried to interrupt him to show their wares for *Belle of New York*. Fred, wearing curling 'Arabian Nights' dancing shoes for his latest picture, agreed to lend an ear. As the score was played over, and Fred chewed gum while he thought, he remained noncommital. Finally, a little while later, it was announced that if Fred did do another film for MGM, it would be *Belle of New York* and he would then fulfil the remainder of his contract. Otherwise, everybody was resigned to the fact that he was on the threshold of retirement.

For the moment, however, he was devoting his worries to *Yolanda And The Thief*. It was a story about a mythical South American country called Patria – 'a cemetery with a train running through it', as Fred describes it in his role as the thief who thinks he can trick the country's richest woman (Lucille Bremer) out of her possessions. The best part of the film was Fred's dancing with Miss Bremer in a ballet sequence, and the comedy of Frank Morgan, ideally cast as another con-man.

Backstage during the shooting of Yolanda and the Thief, *playing backgammon with Lucille Bremer.*

One reviewer said the film looked as though it had dance routines designed by Salvador Dali. All in all, not an Astaire film to remember with particular affection.

Yolanda And The Thief might well have been the film he retired on had there not come a frenzied call from Paramount Studios, where Bing Crosby was struggling through a new film – based, yet again, around the music of Irving Berlin. The trouble was that Bing wasn't getting on at all well with Paul Draper, the leading male dancer in the picture, *Blue Skies*. Draper was meant to be dancing with the attractive female lead, Joan Caulfield and to share a great deal of the banter with Crosby. But it wasn't working out that way. He had a slight stammer, which didn't seem to matter on Broadway, where he had appeared in a number of shows and had always managed to control its worst effects. But nothing seemed to go right on the *Blue Skies* set.

To make things even more difficult, tragedy struck the unit soon after the film got under way. Mark Sandrich, the man who was as responsible as anyone for smoothing the path for Fred Astaire in Hollywood, was appointed producer and director – but quite suddenly, at the age of forty-five, died of a heart attack soon after work on the picture started. Draper was even less confident with the new director, Stuart Heisler– and with Sol C. Siegel who took over as producer – than he had been under Sandrich.

Choosing Fred Astaire to succeed Paul Draper was an inspired move and Fred had no compunction about taking over from another actor. In this case, he wasn't second choice in the conventional sense of the term.

No one else, in fact, could have made a Berlin duet with Crosby seem so perfectly made-to-measure for themselves. 'A Couple of Song And Dance Men' would undoubtedly have become their signature tune had Bing and Fred decided to form a permanent duet. The fact that they didn't can only be the public's loss.

Until *Blue Skies*, another Berlin tune had been principally associated with Harry Richman. After the film, it was as much Fred Astaire as 'Top Hat' had been. 'Puttin' On The Ritz', in fact, was Fred in the old style – almost as if by donning top hat, white tie and tails to sing this number he was signalling the end of war and austerity and saying that he was back in business. Instead, he was still saying that it was his swan song. Hermes Pan had been on war service and Fred brought him back to directing the dance routines in the picture. Between them they devised a backdrop for 'Puttin' On The Ritz' that would have done credit to the most lavish scenes in the Astaire-Rogers series. By a clever special effects, Fred appeared to dance in front of seven other Fred Astaires, all dancing separately.

As for the story, it was no more important than Fred Astaire film plots had ever been. But when there was Crosby to tease and Berlin numbers to which they could sing and dance it mattered even less than usual. For the record, it was about a pair of vaudeville artists who split up; one to continue dancing, the other to run a succession of night clubs. It covered the period 1919 to 1946 – or from 'I've Got My Captain Working For Me Now' to 'White Christmas' and beyond.

The film was a tremendous success – and Mark Sandrich would have approved his successor's change of cast. Surely now, everyone seemed to be asking, Fred would relent and forget about retiring? But Fred said No, he would not forget.

Soon after the film was released in September 1946, the public – aided no doubt by an astute publicity department at Paramount – made it quite clear they didn't like the idea of losing Fred Astaire from their screens. A mammoth petition was launched – collecting signatures day after day in theatre after theatre. After two weeks, the management at New York's Paramount Theatre announced they had 10,000 names written on two rolls of paper, both 50 ft long and 18 inches wide.

'It will be sent to Mr Astaire,' said the manager, 'as the biggest petition of this kind ever presented to anyone.'

If that was something of a publicity stunt, and the public reaction couldn't be completely put down to that, there was not much doubt about the attitude of the city council at Omaha, Nebraska. The leading citizens of Fred's old home town launched their own petition to beg Astaire to reconsider his decision to pack it all in.

He was even more speechless than usual when faced with a mass of praise from ordinary people. 'I am a little surprised and gratified,' he said. 'I had no idea this was going to happen.'

'I thought the public's reaction would be – "Oh well, we don't have to worry with him any more." '

But it wasn't. The clamour for more Astaire snowballed. Even the equally shy Irving Berlin joined in. 'If Fred can be persuaded to make another picture, I'll be glad to write the songs for it,' he declared.

Fred said he took that, too, as a 'terrific compliment'. But he was still retiring. 'I've had a pretty full career in show business – I worked hard in every picture and I was beginning to think the public was becoming a little indifferent.'

What was really worrying Fred – and he never needed any encouragement to worry – was how long he could maintain the standard that had engendered such comments. It wasn't simply that he was tired of hoofing and all it entailed.

'I've tried to fashion something new for each picture,' he told the *Los Angeles Times*, 'But after all, there is a limit. I've never found it easy to perform routines thought up by others. Lately, the feeling has been that people might be saying: "Jeepers – there's old Astaire again, keeps creeping in." '

So what was Fred going to do? Direct? Perhaps. But first he had a little business venture to get under way.

Going over a score with Frank Morgan.

After their great success in Holiday Inn, *Paramount again teamed Fred with Bing Crosby in* Blue Skies. *Here they do the number "A Couple of Song and Dance Men."*

The stars of Blue Skies. *From top to bottom: Billy De Wolfe, Olga San Juan, Joan Caulfield, and Fred.*

Blue Skies *told the story of an eternal triangle—Fred and Bing both pursue Joan Caulfield. Bing wins.*

That there were commercial possibilities with the name Fred Astaire no one could deny. Just by lending his name to a dress hire firm, he could have made a fortune – but he never would. And, as we have seen already, when a firm did try to cash in on the best-dressed man in Hollywood for an advertisement, the legal feathers began to fly as high as those on a dress worn by Ginger Rogers.

But now he was taking a different attitude. He announced he was opening the Fred Astaire Dance Studios, with the first one on New York's smart Park Avenue, the thoroughfare he had sung about so reverently in 'Puttin' On The Ritz'. Later, he said, there would be more and this was going to mark the emergence of the new Fred Astaire, Astaire the businessman.

It wouldn't take long before Fred would get very disenchanted with the dance studio business, but for now, with no film commitments to distract him, he was playing the perfectionist. The launch was going ahead with Astaire-like precision.

There would, he announced, be schools in Kansas, Los Angeles, San Francisco and then London. The whole venture was said to be aiming at beating Arthur Murray on his home ground – and since Mr Murray cashed in to the tune of $20 million a year, that was wishful thinking indeed.

As for Fred, even at the beginning, he found a lot more excitement on the race track. And most of it was called Triplicate.

With his mother, watching Triplicate run.

Few would have guessed that Fred Astaire would be happy in retirement. But it seemed he was. If people had seriously believed that he needed to worry to feel inwardly satisfied, a quick glance at the Astaire household in 1946 would have put them wise.

Mr Twinkletoes – as most writers had dubbed him at least once in the career they had seemingly made out of simply recording his dancing successes – was king of his own little domain: the house at Summit Drive, its 'colony' at Aiken and the Astaire ranch.

Phyllis was quite obviously the consort treated as every inch the queen, a role Fred would have gladly assigned her even had she not figured in the Social Register. As for the children, Peter, Fred Junior and four-year-old Ava – they were the healthy, happy and the devoted subjects of them both.

The $6,000 Fred had spent on buying this three-year-old colt was paying the sort of dividends that would gladden a bank manager's heart. In 1946, he won the Hollywood Gold Cup – a $100,000 race, of which $81,000 went to Fred, together with $6,000 picked up as the result of his betting on the winner. How could he do anything else?

In the same year, he won the $75,000 Golden Gate Handicap in San Francisco and the prestigious San Juan Capistrano at Santa Anita. That was worth $50,000.

Triplicate's success was to last for two years, but finally the horse suffered severe ankle trouble and went off to be a stud in Kentucky. Meanwhile, Fred was beginning to feel as though he were put out to graze himself. It was pleasant enough having nothing to do, but in the house he would still put on his record player and find himself dancing steps he usually liked getting paid for doing.

The fact that an offer came to do just that again was due mainly to Gene Kelly deciding to play a game of volley ball.

Kelly was a different sort of dancer to Astaire; much happier in a pair of jeans and a sweater than in top hat, white tie and tails – and his style went with the dress. If Fred was the suave, urbane gentleman, Gene was the tough stevedore. And, remember it was Astaire who said that dancing was as tough as stevedoring.

But they both were athletes and they both achieved stardom. While Fred confined his athletic prowess to the studio floor or the golfcourse, and indoor sporting activities around his pool table, Kelly loved fast ball games. On this one occasion, playing in the grounds of his own house, he raced a little too hard for the ball, fell down and a couple of players stepped on top of him. Kelly couldn't get up again. His ankle was broken.

To a dancer, breaking an ankle can be as dangerous and foreboding as it is for a racehorse. Gene's injury this time wasn't as serious as it might have been. But it did have repercussions – not just for him, but also for MGM. And for Fred Astaire.

Kelly had been signed to make another film based on the songs of Irving Berlin to be called *Easter Parade*. Now what were they to do?

Offscreen, Fred was a devoted horseman. Here, he is shown with his three-year-old, Triplicate, winner of over a quarter of a million dollars in purses.

Producer Arthur Freed burst into tears when he heard the news. The studio wanted to get on with the making of the picture, but Kelly would be out of action for two months at least – and probably more. In Hollywood two months represents a great deal of capital. Judy Garland was to be the co-star with him – and she could be a difficult lady to work with. In the end, the studio decided that it had to go ahead without Kelly. At Gene's suggestion, a telephone call was made to Fred, who confirmed that he was now out of retirement.

With Triplicate and daughter Ava.

With Phyllis at the races.

Fred protested that he had never really intended to retire completely. He had merely wanted to have a rest from organising dance routines, which always had to be different for every number in every picture. The way he reckoned it, eighty per cent of the effort in creating the routines went into the process of thinking up the steps and only twenty per cent into the job of actually doing them.

But now, with his mental retirement complete, he was having to flex his muscles and see whether he could get to grips with actually moving his feet to the rhythms of Irving Berlin's music.

The man who wrote the story, Sidney Sheldon, wasn't all that delighted at the prospect of having Astaire step into Kelly's dancing shoes – and not simply because it would inevitably mean that a number of Gene's lines and the situations surrounding them would have to be replaced.

It was after Fred had agreed to take on the role that Sheldon was first told. Arthur Freed called the writer to his office and said: 'Guess what's happened? Gene Kelly has broken his ankle.'

'That's very funny, Arthur,' he replied.

'No really,' Freed insisted. What was more, he told him, there were going to be no postponements. 'No. We're starting on Monday. I've sent a script to Fred Astaire.'

When a writer hears that the man he had in his mind's eye all the time that he sat before his typewriter is not going to be the one to say his lines, he is likely to get somewhat disturbed. Sheldon was. He protested that forty-eight-year-old Fred was old enough to be Judy's father. 'Fred's so much older that you could never get an audience rooting for them,' he said.

But Freed was adamant. Sheldon now admits that he was wrong. 'Part of the reason,' he says, 'was that two very talented people were working together and the chemistry was right.'

Gene Kelly's ankle was not the only bone to break in the preliminary stages of *Easter Parade* and so alter the final complexion of the picture. Cyd Charisse had been selected to play Astaire's 'junior' partner in the picture. But she broke a leg, too. At that appropriate moment, Ann Miller – who had been flexing her own long legs at Columbia Pictures for the previous few years and was one of the loveliest dancers in motion pictures, was newly out of hospital after suffering a fall herself. Would she like to test for the role? Miss Miller was jealous of her reputation – as were most performers who had ever had their names above the title in film billings – and refused. That made Fred as worried as usual. He thought she might be too tall for the part. But as far as she was concerned, a pair of flat shoes would solve the perennial problem of girls who had to dance with Fred Astaire – and the studio accepted the suggestion.

In the end, Fred had three dances with Ann Miller, three with Judy, and another two without the benefit of female company.

No one connected with the picture thought it was going to be a walk-over. After twenty films, the man's reputation for perfection had preceded him, and while it was a thrill for most people to be in the same room as Fred Astaire, it was a daunting prospect, too. It extended even to his co-star.

For Judy Garland, *Easter Parade* represented a severe test. Only weeks before arriving on the MGM lot, she had smashed a bathroom mirror and made an attempt at cutting her wrists with the broken glass. She had been under psychiatric care for some time. If that in itself wasn't a big enough problem to wrestle with, there was the additional pressure of seeing her husband replaced as the picture's director – for very personal reasons. Judy's psychiatrist had told MGM that the effect of having Vincente Minnelli directing her in *Easter Parade* could be catastrophic. To her, he wouldn't simply be a husband, but would represent the power of the studio, and little frightened her more than the stern parent figure of MGM. Charles 'Chuck' Walters was brought in in his place.

Judy had worked with Fred before – in the Victory Cavalcade, but now was petrified at the prospect of dancing with him in front of the cameras.

On the first day of any film, there was an atmosphere of excitement and expectancy. There was a tradition at the time that everybody involved in making the picture should see the first take completed and safely locked away in the can. On *Easter Parade*, the atmosphere was electric. It would be Judy's first picture since her much publicised illness and would mark Irving Berlin's forty years of songwriting. But most important of all, it was Fred Astaire's comeback picture.

The plot was in many ways little more than an excuse for Berlin's music and Astaire's dancing. But it was still stronger than most of the ones in which Fred had been involved. He and Ann Miller were a show biz partnership, broken up when Ann decides she wants to go it alone.

In pique, Fred looks for someone else. He finds her in the chorus of a small night club and offers to do for her what Henry Higgins achieved for Eliza Doolittle. Judy – or Hannah Brown as she is called in this picture – has as many fraught problems as the cockney flower girl in *Pygmalion* but, like her, finally comes to appreciate her 'creator'.

The story and the dance scenes seemed to fuse perfectly together. Sidney Sheldon had written the tale around the music numbers and left it to Fred to decide what he wanted to dance and how. But there were complications in some of the scenes involving Fred Astaire, the actor. Early on in the production, Sheldon had an urgent call to meet Astaire on the set. Fred said he couldn't possibly do a scene the way the writer had planned it. He wanted it rewritten.

Fred was supposed to tell Ann Miller just how angry he was at being deserted. Earlier in the story, he had turned down the chance of going to Broadway without her, and now she was accepting a solo part that would leave him out in the cold.

Behind the scenes at the shooting of Easter Parade.

Easter Parade. *Left to right: Ann Miller, Fred and Judy Garland.*

Easter Parade *(1948) brought together the prodigious talents of Fred and Judy Garland, who went from chorus girl to star in the film.*

'I can't do it,' Fred explained, 'because in this scene I'm supposed to be rude to her.'

Fred Astaire, the gallant gentleman, was worried not so much about his image as about the very idea of being rude to a lady.

All in all, *Easter Parade* worked splendidly, relations between star and writer apart. The film was set in the heart of the pre-1917 ragtime era, with mentions of Ziegfeld and Dillingham to evoke memories of Fred's own days on the boards. The tunes ranged from 'I Want To Go Back to Michigan' to 'The Girl on the Magazine Cover' – with 'Easter Parade' itself and an additional batch of sufficient new songs as were considered necessary to keep the whole piece alive and fresh – which is exactly what it turned out to be.

Fred sang and danced: 'It Only Happens When I Dance With You' and Judy Garland heard Peter Lawford tell her he was simply 'A Fella With An Umbrella'. But the real show stopper was a number that owes itself more to Irving Berlin than anyone else. The production was already well in hand when Berlin turned to Arthur Freed and suggested simply 'Let's have a tramps' number'. When Freed said 'Yes,' Berlin produced one of those songs that becomes a milestone in so many different people's lives – as well as a classic piece of cinema. 'A Couple of Swells' actually had the suave Mr Astaire with a tooth blacked out, wearing a filthy frayed collar, a patched tail coat, dirty shoes, a two-day growth of beard and – believe it, you must – a top hat that had probably not been in one piece for a generation. Everybody loved it – especially Judy who was dressed almost identically.

The *New York Times* had just one wish: 'Let's hope that he'll never again talk of retiring.'

To put the paper's mind at rest – and those of a few million fans, too – MGM quickly announced that Fred Astaire would make another big MGM musical and that Judy would again be the co-star. She and Fred were not dancing partners, much more two individual stars who happened to be working in the same picture together, and, as Sheldon said, the chemistry was right.

The new film was to be called *The Barkleys of Broadway* and everyone was certain that Astaire and Garland would make a brilliant job of it. The story was written by Betty Comden and Adolph Green, who always seemed to have a very nice double-act together – reading the script to the assembled company at the beginning of a film.

Judy commented to Fred after the first of these: 'If we can only do as well as they did, we're OK.' Unfortunately, Judy wasn't OK. She started putting on weight and she was constantly ill. The old mental depression that had taken her to a nursing home before *Easter Parade* was back.

Plans had not advanced very far before the studio made the momentous announcement that Judy Garland was going to be replaced. And followed it with a still more momentous statement: the replacement would be Ginger Rogers.

It seemed an incredible, if inspired, choice. A telegram had gone off to Ginger's ranch at Oregon and she had accepted not just a part in a film called *The Barkleys Of Broadway*, but the role of once more being Fred Astaire's partner.

Of course, the news set the gossip columnists into their favourite state of apoplexy. There was going to be one more glorious episode in the Hollywood story labelled 'Astaire–Rogers' and everyone knew how much the two loved the idea of working together again.

That was certainly the popular impression. The old, frequently quoted stories of disagreement between Fred and Ginger were completely forgotten and nobody tried to dig them up from the morgue. In short, the old team were back in harness again – even if neither of them now liked the term any more than they had a decade earlier.

MGM naturally thought that anything RKO could manage in the thirties, they would be able to achieve at the very end of the forties – and if it worked, well, who knew what could be made to happen in the fifties? They certainly knew the value of the Astaire–Rogers combination. Even in pre-war box office terms, when people paid just pennies to see films, RKO's take from the series was an estimated eighteen million dollars.

Certainly, no one was more excited about the prospect of what looked like being an historic moment than Charles Walters, whom producer Arthur Freed had selected to direct the comeback picture. He looked forward to it with all the enthusiasm of a small boy about to be taken to the zoo.

Fred himself has always protested that he and Ginger got on splendidly. They did their work together without rancour and with a professional approach. They respected each other's search for perfection. Ginger has persistently denied that they were anything but the best of friends.

But there is not much doubt either that Fred was slightly less enthusiastic about this pairing than he was willing to admit. The RKO pictures were things that had already happened and he was now developing his acute dislike of dwelling on the past.

But the serious problems came in the wake of Judy Garland's dismissal from the project. One day, Judy turned up at the studio while Ginger was working and somehow managed to break through the security cordon and get on to *The Barkleys* set. She stood behind the camera muttering until ordered to leave by Walters. When she refused to go, he forcibly removed her – as she shouted not particularly nice things at Miss Rogers.

None of the difficulties, however, prevented *The Barkleys of Broadway* from being both a successful and an entertaining film.

Harry Warren wrote a delightful score for the picture and Ira Gershwin provided a set of lyrics that were as good as any he had produced in his entire career. For the big dance number, Ira suggested resurrecting a piece he had written with his brother George – 'They

The famous Barkleys of Broadway *number, "Shoes with Wings On," where Fred, playing a shoemaker, gets snowed under with dancing shoes that mysteriously come to life.*

Can't Take That Away From Me'. No one wanted to take that away from the film.

The story was much less flimsy than the others had been – although the trend for this had already been set with the last film, *The Castles.* Newspaper reports said the new picture was based on the life of the celebrated actress Gaby Deslys. Certainly, one incongruous part of the picture comes when Ginger takes it into her head to do a Sarah Bernhardt – and recites the Marseillaise to a stunned but appreciative *Academie Francaise.*

Charles Walters has misty eyes when he insists that Fred and Ginger seemed to love each other in front of the cameras – and a misty memory. Basically, the Barkleys were almost always at war with each other. They were a married dance team who were constantly quarrelling. He wanted her to continue dancing; she wanted a dramatic career – the irony of that situation didn't strike many people at the time, but it was just the sort of thing being reported at the time newsmen were speculating in the thirties, about the Astaire–Rogers partnership's future.

At forty-nine, Astaire had lost none of his skill afoot, vocally or as a comedian.

Ginger was spotted at a preview of the picture and proved that she hadn't lost any of her old nerves. She sat entirely still throughout the whole film without muttering a word to her companion, although she occasionally seemed to be mopping her brow.

Just as in the old days, everybody wanted to know what the next Astaire–Rogers film would be. There was indeed talk of more, but it dwindled away. No plans were actually announced, and there was to be no eleventh Astaire–Rogers film. The two had done what the fans had been begging for, and once done, it was enough.

The Barkleys of Broadway *reunited Fred and Ginger, but the old magic was gone, replaced by nostalgia. The movie was written by a young team, Betty Comden and Adolph Green.*

So what now? It was the question asked every time any one had ever mentioned the ending of the partnership with Ginger previously, and it was again the question in 1949. Now it seemed less important, because the film industry had changed and the film musical had altered with it. As for Fred Astaire, at the turn of his half-century, he seemed very happy indeed with the way things were.

There was a polish to the screen that it had lacked before, and the dancing and singing were both sophisticated and more real, both of which pleased Mr Astaire very greatly.

The question of partners continued to crop up, but there was devastating news about his next film. He was going to stop dancing before the picture was halfway through. His new partner in the picture would be Red Skelton. The film turned out to be *Three Little Words* which was to prove the first of a glorious series in an even more glorious Astaire decade.

It was different from anything Fred had done before. There would be more comedy than previously and because he stops dancing so early on in the scenario, more acting opportunities for him, too. It once again had Fred in a biographical role – playing songwriter Bert Kalmar to Skelton's Harry Ruby. Such dancing as Fred did do was opposite a little charmer who was to make a fair impact on Hollywood in the fifties, Vera-Ellen (the hyphen was always used in her billing).

Much of the glamor in the picture revolved around the beauty – she was, in fact, a beauty consultant as well as an actress – Arlene Dahl, although her big number threatened to turn into a reprise of what was not exactly Fred Astaire's happiest memory of the films with Ginger Rogers.

She stood at the top of a large staircase with a pink fan, frightened above all else of falling off and crashing to the ground. She was also frightened of sneezing, for with every step she took, more feathers from the fan flew in all directions. One or two of them lingered around her nose for so long that she was certain a calamity was imminent.

When she finally did reach the ground, with Astaire ready to sweep her firmly off her feet, there were a few whispered words of comfort from him too which was calculated to put any leading lady at ease.

Fred's dancing exploits in the picture end when Bert Kalmer is supposed to have a serious fall and takes to songwriting with his baseball addict partner Harry Ruby. In between, there are the usual jokes, the usual girls – one of them a delightful young lady called Debbie Reynolds – and the usual love story. The tunes, all by Ruby and Kalmar, were standards like 'I Wanna Be Loved By You', 'Nevertheless', 'Who's Sorry Now', 'You Are My Lucky Star' and the title tune. There was also the added benefit of the occasional period piece like 'So long – Oolong'.

Fred certainly liked making *Three Little Words* and the box office

Three Little Words teamed Fred with yet another partner, Vera-Ellen.

In Three Little Words, *Fred plays lyricist Bert Kalmar, who, with his baseball-mad partner Harry Ruby (Red Skelton), produced such hits as "I Wanna Be Loved by You," and "Three Little Words."*

take proved he had chosen a pretty good vehicle for himself. The critics apparently thought so, too. The New York *Herald Tribune* said that both Astaire and Vera-Ellen were 'at the top of their form'. It was a sentiment echoed by most American writers.

Every now and again, Fred worried as much as the critics about the rash of so-called screen biographies – *Three Little Words* contained the occasional germ of truth but hardly worried itself about mere facts. In an age when true stories of people who could be given some kind of musical peg were being rushed to the studios as quickly as they could be dashed off the typewriter, approaches were made to Fred, too – to agree to have someone play *him* in a film. It was basically an academic question for the future, since Astaire was still working and his face was known to every small boy on both sides of the Atlantic. But studios liked to buy options – if only to prevent their competitors making a picture first.

Fred said 'No' – just as everybody expected him to do. When five years before, Warner Brothers had made the George Gershwin story *Rhapsody In Blue*, the young dancer friend of the composer was given an entirely meaningless name, although most people suspected it was meant to be Astaire. Soon after *Three Little Words* was released, Fred inserted a clause in his will. He directed that no one should ever attempt to make a film biography of him.

About this time, he said of his own film appearances: 'When I see myself on the screen, I'm immediately sorry about the whole business. I want to get up and walk out. And sometimes I do.'

Now he wanted to protect future generations from the same sort of 'suffering'.

Most of all he wanted to protect his private life. By now he and Phyllis had achieved what everybody told them would be impossible. They had kept the public away from their front door. By avoiding the razzamataz and steering clear of the big public occasions, Fred could live two distinct lives.

When he and Phyllis did entertain or go out for dinner the evenings were as private as those anyone outside Hollywood enjoyed in their own homes. Frequently, the David Nivens and the Astaires dined with each other. Often, it was the Astaires and the Cole Porters.

Fred also kept up his interest in the dance schools although he spent much less time on them than previously. He had about forty of these now, the largest was the one in New York and there were plans to continue expanding.

If Fred ever felt that he could be dancing faster or playing better – or even just that he wished he had never made a picture at all – the emotions were all applicable to his next movie, *Let's Dance*. Even Hermes Pan has allowed himself to suggest that Fred should have saved his effort and done something else. Betty Hutton was teamed with him in this and as Pan and everyone else agrees, it was miscasting of the classic sort. Fred insists he and Betty Hutton got along fine but others sensed some tension.

Fred needed to dance with a graceful lady, but Betty Hutton was used to exercising her lungs like a female Tarzan.

There were, however, occasional moments of delight even in *Let's Dance*, the best of them featuring Astaire the piano player as much as Astaire the dancer; in one scene he showed just what an adept dab hand at the keyboard he could be. He didn't merely play the piano, he danced around it, to the accompaniment of a cat's chorus. It was Hermes Pan's idea to stuff ten cats inside the piano and release them only when the number was completed!

The number apart, *Let's Dance* was a disaster and looking back today from afar, it was the only hiatus in those glorious Fifties. *Royal Wedding* which opened in February 1951 was more in the usual romantic Astaire niche. The story of a Broadway brother and sister dance team who come to London in time for the marriage of the then Princess Elizabeth and Prince Philip was right up Fred's street.

Of course, there was a distinct similarity to the story of Fred and Adele, the film brother and sister take a show to the elegant British capital and the girl falls in love with a peer of the realm. And as in the film version of the one show Fred didn't do with Adele, there were title problems with *Royal Wedding*. As *Gay Divorce* became *Gay Divorcee* in America, so *Royal Wedding* became *Wedding Bells* in Britain – the British were thought to be rather sensitive about the use of the word 'royal'.

As in countless other Astaire pictures there were also casting problems. Selected to play Fred's sister was June Allyson, the nearest Hollywood had come to a 'Sweetheart' since Mary Pickford. And by all accounts she revelled in the idea. Matters were complicated, however, when she became pregnant.

As a result of this inconvenience, MGM tried to show that, despite all that had happened in the past, it had a heart. The studio boldly announced that Judy Garland would play with Fred Astaire again – and so give everyone the opportunity of enjoying once more the duo who had made such an impact in *Easter Parade*. But that, too, was more easily said than done. Chuck Walters was relieved of the task of directing the picture because he said he couldn't face the agony of another Astaire–Garland project. He knew what he was doing.

Judy started turning up late for rehearsals and then began missing them out altogether. Before long, she was summarily dismissed just as she had been from *The Barkleys*.

Judy's dismissal came by telegram – a long, meandering legal document sent to every one of half a dozen addresses where she was considered likely to be staying. It was the end of any notion that she and Fred would make a good investment for MGM and more good entertainment for the public.

Films like shows, however, have to go on. The choice for Fred's partner finally settled on Jane Powell who sang and danced beautifully, and because she was about eight inches shorter than Fred, presented not the slightest problem of being seen in close-up with him.

Fred and Phyllis at a Hollywood night spot. In September, 1954, Phyllis died of a brain tumor, ending what has been called "the most perfect Hollywood marriage." Fred was affected very deeply.

Let's Dance *(1950) was one of those movies that most people agreed should never have been made. Not only did Fred and co-star Betty Hutton have incompatible screen styles, but there were also rumors that the two didn't get along very well.*

In Royal Wedding, *one of the best-known numbers featured Fred dancing on the floor, walls and ceiling of his hotel room. In reality, the scene was shot in a room that revolved, and Fred never really left the floor.*

Royal Wedding *tells the story of a brother-sister dance team (Fred and Jane Powell) who go to England and both fall in love. It was loosely based on the experience of Fred and Adele.*

The Belle of New York *again teamed Fred with Vera-Ellen.*

In 1951, Fred was presented with a special Oscar for "the artistry that has brought a unique delight to picture audiences and has raised the standards of all musical pictures." He was unable to receive the award in person, so Ginger Rogers accepted it in his place. Here, he is shown with George Murphy.

Alan Jay Lerner, who wrote the screenplay and the lyrics, was not as overawed by what he had created as were a number of people who sat in canvas-backed chairs on film sets. He said he was frightened that the picture was going to charm itself to death.

One of the numbers in the film that prevented that happening was a comedy tour-de-force that deserves to be re-run whenever anyone has the bright idea of showing a history of the movie musical. It is all summed up by the title 'How Could You Believe Me When I Said I Loved You When You Know I've Been A Liar All My Life'. Astaire and Jane Powell sing it in one of the film's stage interludes and time after time it set audiences clapping – which is normally a pretty unrewarding thing to do in a cinema. But the fact that the screen can neither hear nor react didn't stop it happening. Burton Lane and Lerner created the number in the course of a short car journey. Lerner mentioned the title in one breath of inspiration and Lane just happened to hum the tune.

Fred danced in this film in nightclubs, on a stage and in a gymnasium – where he did one of his most famous routines with the least temperamental partner of his whole career, a hat stand. But the dance that made people positively hold on to their seats was one in a small room. Fred seemed to dance like a fly on the ceiling and, without support, on the windows and walls too. 'How on earth is that done?' people were supposed to ask – and for the most part they did. The secret has since been revealed – although never satisfactorily copied. Fred danced in a room that formed part of a revolving drum. Since the camera went round with the rest of the drum, the audiences were left with the illusion that Fred was actually dancing upside down and sideways. Clever stuff, indeed.

Despite the critics' general lack of enthusiasm for *Royal Wedding*, Fred was given a token of appreciation for his contribution to motion pictures and from the people who knew best of all how important that contribution had been—the film industry, itself. They presented him with a special Oscar, marking his outstanding part in the Hollywood story. Appropriately, the award was accepted by Ginger Rogers, as Fred was out of town when the presentation ceremony took place.

The citation for the Oscar stated that it was given for 'the artistry that has brought a unique delight to picture audiences and has raised the standards of all musical pictures'.

If Vera-Ellen, as the critic had said, was the natural successor to Miss Rogers, the ticket-buyers were invited to show their approval or disapproval of the fact in Fred's next film.

Together they made *The Belle of New York* the movie Astaire was due to film just before he announced his temporary retirement in 1946. It was the film he had promised Arthur Freed he would do should he ever come out of that retirement. The five pictures that preceded it seemed to indicate that he constantly tried to put it off.

Fred never liked *Belle* and, after it was made, neither did many of the critics. But like *Royal Wedding* it looks very much better today than it did at the time—and the songs by Harry Warren and Johnny Mercer were both tuneful and good. It was very loosely based on the old Broadway show and the story was set in that same turn-of-the-century era, but there were a number of 'fifties hallmarks about it and altogether the film deserves a better fate than it has ever enjoyed. The principal weaknesses are in the crude attempts at trick photography and a few hints from *The Barkleys of Broadway* in that direction would not have gone amiss.

Vera-Ellen, like all the Astaire leading ladies at one time or another, was somewhat in awe of Fred. And like all the others, she was amazed at just how worried Fred could be over whether or not a number was working out. But she was tickled by another Astaire characteristic, producing pictures of his horses from his wallet in much the same way other men showed photographs of their children. He had quite an extensive stable by now, although none of them looked like being another Triplicate. There were high hopes particularly for Triplicate's younger daughter Stripteaser – hopes that never were to be completely realised.

He was trying to slot *Belle of New York* into the same category, but its failure concerned him just the same. He has said in his autobiography that the only thing *Belle of New York* gave him was a fortune.

Charles Walters did direct this picture and has been even more uncharitable about it than Fred. He said he hated everything about it – and mainly because he didn't think there was any real chemistry between Astaire and Vera-Ellen. I must say the finished result didn't give that impression, and there certainly had been a great deal of that mysterious reaction known as chemistry between them in *Three Little Words*.

Eventually, they got out a completed story. It had several similarities to the original Broadway production which had been the very first American show to come to London's West End – and was about a playboy who falls for a girl Salvationist. But the music was new and so was the dancing in thin air that both Fred and Vera-Ellen did to show they were in love. It was as corny as that – but sometimes corn can be enjoyable and *Belle of New York* is so today.

On the ranch, where the family was now growing oranges and grapefruit as well as raising the horses, Fred was an entirely different man. Stripteaser was fussed over like a baby. If she didn't actually feel like one of the family it was not the fault of any of the Astaires.

The ranch was a superb escape valve, a place where Fred could be the country gentleman who loved to play jazz records or work out on his own set of drums. It was also the place where he could consider all the offers that constantly came in. There was talk soon after the completion of *Belle of New York* of launching him in a new Betty Comden and Adolph Green story called *The Strategy of Love*. The title's pedigree didn't seem the kind of thing Fred Astaire would attempt – it was based on a fourteenth century guide to romance, but was updated as the

An informal photograph of the Astaire family at home. From left to right: Fred, Ava, Fred Jr., and Phyllis.

story of a television writer who attempts to woo a modern young miss.

Ever since the remainder of Fred's hair first began going grey, he had worried about the implications of his dancing with much younger girls. That could be the principal reason he rejected *Strategy Of Love* – despite the entreaties of Arthur Freed and the rest of the MGM hierarchy.

Much more readily, he accepted another Freed production, *The Band Wagon*. That, of course, had been the title of one of his happiest Broadway experiences, the last show he and Adele did together.

There were a few similarities between the stage *Band Wagon* and the film, but not enough to notice. The main one, of course, was the presence of Fred Astaire. The other similarity was in the music. The scores of both were provided by Arthur Schwartz and Howard Dietz. Four of the tunes had, in fact, been in the earlier show – 'High and Low'; 'Dancing In The Dark'; 'New Sun In The Sky' and the merry-go-round German spoof that made such an impact on Broadway in 1931, 'I Love Louisa'. That being said, everything about the new *Band Wagon* was different – and new, in every way.

It was new because the film had a definite plot – about a screen star of the recent past who decides to make a comeback via a Broadway show – while the stage version had been a revue without any pretence of a story. It was importantly new because it linked Astaire with probably his most competent dancing partner to date, and certainly one of the most beautiful, Cyd Charisse. And it was new because it also featured a young lady whose memories of Mr Astaire are neither as pleasant nor as adulatory as those of most of her predecessors.

Nanette Fabray had the second female lead in the picture, she played the young girl writer who, with Oscar Levant, had just completed the very show that would give the star played by Astaire his new break. She sang and danced – and did both charmingly. She acted as though the situations were actually happening instead of merely learning a collection of lines written for her by Betty Comden and Adolph Green. But she and Fred Astaire did not get on – and that is putting it mildly.

The dance director for *Band Wagon* was a little man who at the time was described as symbolising the new young crop of Hollywood geniuses, Michael Kidd. Kidd went on to star in a picture himself, to choreograph and then also to direct a vast number of successful Broadway shows.

It was the uncanny combination of Astaire and Charisse that impressed itself most on Kidd. Uncanny because they really did work together beautifully.

Fred and Cyd had met each other very briefly when they both had taken part in *Ziegfeld Follies* – so briefly that they were on screen for only seconds and Fred had really no reason to remember her at all. It was while she was working on another MGM film that Astaire appeared on the set, without warning and proceeded to walk round and

Watching the action during the filming of The Band Wagon.

round her like a fox sizing up a new prey. In a way that was precisely what Fred was doing. When Arthur Freed offered her the co-starring part in *The Band Wagon* she realised what the circling had all been about. Astaire had simply been trying to work out how tall she was. When the shapely and amazingly beautiful Miss Charisse was established as shorter than he was, the green light was given to the idea of her becoming the latest Astaire dancing partner.

The work on the picture wound up just before Christmas 1952. On the very last day, Nanette Fabray says she went into the studio heavily laden with presents for everyone. But nobody was around to accept them. The way she sees it, the cast and crew just couldn't get shot of it all quickly enough.

Fred was happy enough himself with *The Band Wagon*, in fact he has said it was one of his favourites. As for there being problems with my work, 'I don't have problems in my work. Just solutions!' With his mother and Ava, he and Phyllis celebrated their twentieth wedding anniversary by attending the film's world premiere. It was to be a brief moment of happiness.

Cyd Charisse, one of the most striking dancers in Hollywood was actually upstaged by Fred's dancing during rehearsals. He was then 54 years old.

The stars of The Band Wagon *(minus Cyd Charisse). They are, left to right: Jack Buchanan, Fred, Nanette Fabray, and Oscar Levant.*

Besides Fred, the cast of The Band Wagon *included Nanette Fabray and Jack Buchanan, here shown with Fred doing "Triplets."*

137

If you were outside the film colony, chances are you didn't even know that Mrs Phyllis Astaire existed. A straw poll of film fans would probably have produced a majority vote in favor of Ginger Rogers as the true identity of Mrs Fred Astaire.

But things were to change, and before very long an announcement would go round the world that would shock everyone who heard it.

The first indication that all was not well should have been noticed the day at California's Santa Anita race track when Phyllis asked to be taken home early because of a sudden headache. But she recovered quickly and there didn't seem much point in pursuing the matter.

Then, just before the following Easter and at another race meeting, she felt ill again. A little later on, she was bad enough to call off going to a dinner party given by Cole Porter.

It was after that night that Phyllis went to see her doctor. He ordered X-rays to be taken. On Good Friday 1954, Phyllis had an operation, followed five hours later by a second one. This revealed what Fred had never dared to allow himself to suspect – a brain tumor. But it was never removed, the surgeons decided it was inaccessible. After these traumas, it seemed perhaps that all would be well. Fred Junior was in the Air Force at Texas and after coming home on special leave was told there was no reason not to go back to his base. The Astaires went back to their ranch.

Phyllis had made such good progress that the X-ray treatments she had been prescribed were now curtailed and the nurse who was employed to look after her was sent home.

Then in August 1954, Phyllis was back at the hospital where her first two operations had been carried out. She had had a serious relapse and a new operation was ordered. After surgery, she stayed in a coma for weeks. Finally, on September 14, she died. She was forty-six.

For Fred Astaire, dancer, film actor, singer, best-dressed man in Hollywood, life was blacker than it had ever been before. Up to then, he had seemingly been spared the tragedies of life that befall a lot of people, just as he had been granted far more blessings than most would ever dream possible. Now the blessings were in the past and the future seemed not just bleak, but meaningless.

There was, however, one saving grace: Twentieth Century Fox had signed Fred to make a film and everyone said he should do it.

It wasn't easy to comtemplate smiling in public – let alone laughing as he played the drums to a hot beat. And he would have to do all that in the picture which was to be yet another version of the classic *Daddy Long Legs*. But his friends told him to do it, and he accepted the advice. Having done that, the perfectionist in Fred Astaire wouldn't allow himself to do anything but behave as he would on any other project. It was just what his friends knew would happen. He worked himself until it seemed there could be no more energy left in his body. Cast opposite him was twenty-two-year-old Leslie Caron – she, with the gamin look that became her trade mark, played the young orphan Fred adopts and who knows his identity only by the long shadow of his legs.

It turned out to be one of the best Astaire films ever – and certainly the best version of the story by Jean Webster. It had first seen the light of day, as a very successful play at the Gaiety Theatre, London. Seven years later it was a silent film with Mary Pickford. In 1952, it had its first musical treatment, again in London, but under the title *Love from Judy*.

The Astaire–Caron version, under its original name, had a completely original score by Johnny Mercer, one of the few occasions on which he was able to show his amazing talent for writing both the words and music; the ballet music was by Alec North. The title of one of these tunes became a classic explanation of the effects of the interminable problem of an older man falling for a younger girl, 'Something's Got To Give'. Mercer adopted a very wise scientific rule to form the first line of the song 'When an irresistable force such as you meets an old immovable object like me'. He also produced the number that Fred regards as his favourite above all other songs – 'Dream'.

In addition, there was also a dance that was better known for its music than for its steps, 'The Sluefoot'.

Leslie Caron liked *Daddy Long Legs*. 'For once,' she said, 'I play someone for whom everything smiles.' She had just played a poor waif in the film *Lili*.

The New York *Sunday News* simply said: 'Astaire is still tops as a song-and-dance man.'

As for Fred himself, he was putting on a brave front. But his misery at the loss of Phyllis was taking on a strange form. Other men might have sat at home and moped. Fred did a peculiar thing. He went on an escapade sizing up the local mail boxes – for an illegal purpose. As everywhere else in the United States, the letter boxes near his Beverly Hills home are red and blue. He suddenly had an idea – if he painted the middle of the boxes yellow, they would be in his exact racing colors.

Fred didn't go as far as actually painting the boxes, but he did stick yellow Scotch tape around their midriffs; driving from one box to the next and looking to see who was watching him as he did it.

There are Astaire friends who wondered how he ever took the plunge with Phyllis in the first place as he had always seemed such a loner. And none of them imagined he would now go looking for a replacement, Phyllis was irreplaceable and he knew that their own special brand of marriage was, too. Besides which, there was always the inbred reluctance to admit that the perfect love affair was over. Even now, over twenty years later, there are days when he secretly thinks she is going to walk through the door as though nothing had happened.

When *Daddy Long Legs* was over, there was talk of Fred even shutting himself away from the one place where he had proved he

In Daddy Long Legs, *Fred got to show off another of his many talents, drumming.*

Daddy Long Legs *tells the story of a wealthy businessman (Fred) who anonymously sponsors the education of an orphan girl (Leslie Caron). She fantasizes about her benefactor and falls in love with a man she meets, not realizing they are one and the same.*

could best forget his troubles – the film studio. He made his television debut in 1955 on the Ed Sullivan Show, but that was basically to plug the film and he didn't get paid for the experience.

The rumours of an Astaire retirement were heightened when a big new film for Twentieth Century Fox called *Dry Martini* was mentioned in connection with Fred, but it just never came off.

Then Paramount said they were going to star him in a film to be directed by Jean Negulesco, and written by Henry and Pheobe Ephron, the same trio who were responsible for *Daddy Long Legs*. Like *Daddy*, it would be a musical with Sammy Cahn writing the lyrics to Jimmy Van Heusen's music.

This was to be called *Papa's Delicate Condition* – the delicate condition referred to being the gentleman's appreciation of the delights of the bottle. The film would be based on the life of a man called Jack Griffith, which had been written by his daughter, Corinne Griffith, a silent movie star. As Sammy Cahn told me, it represented a career-long ambition for him – to write for Fred Astaire. He even agreed to audition for the master. When it came to the day they were to demonstrate one of the tunes, Cahn says he was rather more enthusiastic than Van Heusen who regarded the idea of an audition as being beneath his dignity.

But demonstrate it they did. The song was 'Call Me Irresponsible' and it was planned for the moment in the film that the man with the delicate condition was trying to explain to his wife why he had spent so much money on buying a circus – just so that his little girl would be happy.

The pair got halfway through the song, Cahn says in his masterly book *I Should Care*, when Astaire ordered them to stop. Commands from Astaire could never be ignored and when they came, the people involved usually got more than a little worried. This time, the songwriters need not have been too put out – Fred told them it was one of the finest songs he had ever heard. He also revealed why Van Heusen and Cahn had been invited to supply the score, it was because Johnny Mercer was not available.

But neither 'Call Me Irresponsible' nor any of the four or five other songs they wrote for the picture were ever sung by Astaire. In fact *Papa's Delicate Condition* was made without Fred; Jackie Gleason took the role intended for Astaire. The reason given was that Fred had an obligation to MGM to fulfil first. But that took time, too.

For the moment, Fred was still trying to reconcile himself to what was irreconcilable – life without Phyllis. He would wake up at three o'clock in the morning, just about the time when he used to get some of his brightest inspirations, and the depression would hit him deeper than ever before.

The trouble with Fred was that he was in limbo, unable to accept the fact that he was now alone, yet not really sure he could work in the same old way, either. The old haunts that he and Phyllis enjoyed so

Fred and Ava at her coming-out party. Next to them are Anthony Quinn and his daughter, Christina.

much were too painful for him to retain them exclusively for himself. From the time that she died, for instance, he couldn't return to the ranch. When years later he happened to go past the place, the experience was almost unbearable.

Without Phyllis, he was depending on his mother and on Ava for feminine company. In July 1955, the three of them went to Europe on holiday. Ava was thirteen, and he started escorting her to the odd film première – as much a treat for a young girl on the threshold of her teens as company for a star.

In between, Fred had weakened and agreed that perhaps his dancing days were not, after all, over. He consented to make a film for MGM called *Wedding Day* and admitted that the most enticing part of the deal was that he was going to co-star with Audrey Hepburn. Before long, it was decided to change the title to *Funny Face*, like *Band Wagon* an evocative name straight out of the two Astaires' Broadway careers. And also like the film *Band Wagon*, it had very little to do with the original show.

All there was, in fact, to connect the two was the title and the fact that the Gershwins supplied the music. Four of the numbers were taken from the original stage production – 'Funny Face' itself, 'S' Wonderful', 'Let's Kiss And Make Up' and 'He Loves And She Loves'.

Leonard Gershe and Ronald Edens supplied the other tunes which they had originally planned for a Broadway show that never came off. The story was also the one they had planned to put on Broadway under the name 'Wedding Day'.

The path to true success in films, rather like the one to true love, rarely runs smooth. And so it was with what became *Funny Face*. There were impossible contract difficulties getting the picture under way at MGM. Eventually, the whole deal was sold to Paramount, who had had Audrey Hepburn under contract in the first place. Audrey insisted Fred do the picture with her.

It was the story of a fashion photographer who finds what was shortly to become known as a beatnik in Greenwich Village. He takes her to Paris where, of course, all good movies must be photographed. What neither the story nor Paramount took into consideration was the fact that it sometimes rains in Paris. It certainly did when *Funny Face* was being shot. Numbers suddenly had to be given a rainy background where originally no one gave rain a passing thought. And the sun came out only when it was not wanted. It would have been much easier if it kept raining throughout the same scene, but artificial rain had to be created by hose pipes when, obstinately, there was none of the genuine variety.

By far the hardest problem caused by the weather was the effect it had on the dance numbers. On one celebrated occasion an entire area had to be resurfaced with new earth and grass, because everything underneath was waterlogged.

Another problem was controlling the Paris crowds. This was partly solved by dressing some of the extras as gendarmes. One of the people they had to control turned out to be Hermes Pan who was on holiday in Paris and investigating what looked like a familiar scene – without realising who was involved in it. Fred immediately changed Pan's hotel booking so that they could be near each other. It was a great reunion for them.

His big solo in the picture was a complicated bull fight mime – in which he used his raincoat as a cape. But one of the most endearing parts of *Funny Face* was the moment Fred played with his hat. He simply tipped it off his head with a cane. It looked the simplest routine in the world, the sort of thing with which fathers amuse their children at parties. But fastidious Fred Astaire rehearsed it with all his usual dedication.

143

In Funny Face, *Fred plays an American photographer living in Paris who falls in love with Greenwich Village librarian Audrey Hepburn.*

Silk Stockings *brought Fred and Cyd Charisse back together again. It was directed by Rouben Mamoulian, with songs by Cole Porter.*

Fred and Kay Thompson clown it up in Funny Face.

145

Fred did his own choreography including a pas-de-deux with Audrey Hepburn. For her, it was the most important professional dancing she had yet done. Fred danced too, with Kay Thompson, who in a charming character study played the magazine editor.

There was an important historic feature about *Funny Face* – historic, that is, as far as show business is concerned. For the first time, songs from the soundtrack of a film were put on an LP record instead of them being re-recorded later on in another studio.

In 1956, production began on what we now know was the last glamorous film musical of the entire Astaire career, *Silk Stockings*, the film adaptation of a Broadway show which itself was a version of a movie classic. Back in the 1930s Greta Garbo had carved a niche in cinema history by starring in *Ninotchka*, the story of a Russian woman diplomat who is led astray in decadent Paris. Cole Porter had written the score and it all seemed to bode very well when Fred and Cyd Charisse were again dancing together at MGM.

Cyd was excited at being with Fred once more and it seems that he was, too. As a gesture of his appreciation, on the day they began work he presented Cyd with a cage-full of red-billed finches – the red intended to represent the Russian she was playing in the film.

The offer to make *Silk Stockings* came to Cyd Charisse at a moment when fixing her time schedule resembled a juggling act. Her MGM contract was such that she went from one film to the next and had to think about a third before the second was completed.

Producer Arthur Freed did, however, give her a say in the matter. She could, he said, either do *Les Girls* with Gene Kelly or *Silk Stockings* with Fred Astaire. She said there was no contest and chose Astaire. It wasn't just that she was working with Fred again – although that was a very important consideration – but also that she recognised Ninotchka as the best role in her career. She could also see a lot of a man she greatly admired, Cole Porter. Porter told her he would rather have Astaire be the first to sing his songs than anyone else – because only he showed them the care that a songwriter appreciated.

It was obviously a happy combination for Astaire and Charisse. Cyd knew that Fred had the right to approve his partner, and after *The Band Wagon* he knew what he was getting. Even so, Arthur Freed had had his time cut out trying to persuade Fred to take the role in the first place. He just had the feeling that people wouldn't accept him as the romantic lead to a girl so much his junior.

Eventually, at the suggestion of the director, Rouben Mamoulian, Freed arranged a lunch for the three of them. After being wined and lunched, Fred took his pen and signed the contract. The film was going to be made.

Again Miss Charisse's long legs and her beautiful figure made it difficult for eyes to switch to Astaire, yet once more, his dancing persuaded audiences and crew alike that there was still something special in him, too.

Leonard Gershe, who with Leonard Spigelgass, wrote the screenplay, was not altogether sure that casting Fred was totally successful. He said that the conniving film producer who Fred played needed something that he never had – 'commonness'.

The film must go down in history, if only because it was the very last picture in which Fred wore top hat, white tie and tails. Since Astaire always wanted to live in the present, Hermes Pan, now back at work with his old pal, had to persuade him to adopt the costume for a number called 'The Ritz Roll 'N' Rock'. Fred thought the whole outfit was rather passé, but to the people watching it all, it just looked like Fred Astaire – and no one asked for more.

The film also had comedy with the help of Peter Lorre in one of his last and least sinister roles, and Janis Paige as the film star who, incidentally, comes to Paris to make yet another version of *War And Peace*.

It was up to Mamoulian, having solved his casting problems, to decide just what sort of film he wanted it to be. The picture was to be in Cinemascope, which since it was first introduced as the answer to TV had been voted by directors the most difficult medium in which to work. It was an ungainly size, the proportions were all wrong and before long it would be replaced by Panavision and similar systems.

Mamoulian felt that the emphasis had to be on dancing, above all else. And since never again was Fred to be seen on film doing the sort of routines he did with Cyd Charisse in *Silk Stockings* it was a wise choice.

Fred, as usual, worked his taps to a shine – but had enough energy left over to take part in a fake scene which he laid on as a sort of practical farewell present for the director at the end of the filming.

Mamoulian loved working with Astaire. It was, after all, a meeting of two perfectionists. 'You'd think,' he said after *Silk Stockings*, 'that his entire life and future depended on the outcome of each dance. He keeps at the top because he does the impossible. He improves on perfection.'

For once, Fred himself revealed a secret of his craft. 'It's always murder to get that easy effect,' he said. 'I don't try to make things look easy. I'd like them to look hard so that people would know what work went into them.'

It certainly impressed Arthur Freed: 'The man is absolutely ageless,' he told reporters when the film was safely in the can, 'Why, I'm only a couple of years older than he is and I look like his grandfather! After only three hours, I'm ready to drop. I've been so exhausted that they thought they'd have to give me oxygen. Fred just looks at me and tells me to rest and keeps on dancing for six hours more.'

But now, at the end of the 1950s, Astaire's public wouldn't believe that he could be out of step with their tastes, and they were still wanting more. Over the past seven years, in fact, he had been showing a newer, more up-to-date image, and when you talked to him, you knew there was still a lot more he wanted to do.

Of all Fred's partners following the breakup with Ginger Rogers in 1939, none had the impact of Barrie Chase, whom he teamed up with in 1958. Fred and Barrie overwhelmed television audiences in their special, "An Evening With Fred Astaire."

It was a new world. The war was now fading as a memory and a whole new generation of people made up the audiences for entertainers like Astaire; people who were just children when he was dancing for the troops, who were not born when he and Ginger were the most popular stars on the screen. They were now the ones who seemed to have this changing world at their feet.

They had money, they spent fortunes on records, on going to the movies and on buying the first color television sets. For Fred Astaire, feeding those sets became a notion he found difficult to resist.

His plans were still topics for conversation. Would he retire again? And, more important still, would he marry again? The answers were slightly more evasive to the first question than those to the second. He had no doubts at all about his personal life. 'I had one of the happiest marriages a man could want,' he said. 'For twenty-two years, it ran and when it closed, when I lost her, I couldn't work up an interest in anyone else.'

But what about television? Now, he did appear to be weakening in that direction. He followed up his appearance with Ed Sullivan with stints on the Arlene Francis and Art Linkletter shows. On the Person-to-Person program, he once more showed his talent with the drums. But Marie Torre in the New York *Herald Tribune* reluctantly prophesied that this was merely a passing fad, not something Fred was likely to take as a spur for the future.

'The recent Fred Astaire appearances on television,' she wrote, 'have sprung hope in the hearts of video pursuers who have been falling over antennae trying to shake loose from the movie lots. Sad to relate, however, any TV man with Astaire in his eyes is merely having a pipe dream.' And Fred certainly did seem to be saying as much himself. Ask him why he did make his excursions on to the small screen and he would reply disarmingly: 'I like to visit my friends.'

Then, in August 1957, came the news that both Fred and Charles Laughton had been hooked by CBS. They would each star in a General Electric Theatre film. Fred's would be a comedy fantasy by Jameson Brewer called *Imp On A Cobweb Leash*.

It was aired in December that year and was well received. In fact, so well received that Fred decided that for the first time he was going to think very seriously indeed about yet another new career – in television – possibly even doing his own thing on the medium, dancing.

Matters came to a head when Astaire and the Chrysler Corporation reached an agreement that opened up entirely new vistas for a man who began entertaining in the first decade of the century. Chrysler agreed to package a television programme that would go out live and in colour. As for Fred, he would not only star in it, but produce the show, too – under the banner of his newly-formed company Ava Productions.

It was at that point that history looked as if it were about to repeat itself. Who, everyone wanted to know, would be . . . yes . . . Fred's partner? When he told them, the headline writers inevitably described

her as the new Ginger Rogers. Fred could have told them they would do that but restrained himself.

But in many ways, for once, they were right. Fred had selected a young girl whom he always agrees was one of his most accomplished partners. She was also one of the youngest and one of the most beautiful. Her name – Barrie Chase.

Fred had first noticed Barrie when she had had a small supporting role in *Silk Stockings*. Blonde, very slim and short enough to make Fred look tall, she was enchanting and also very hard working. The daughter of writer Borden Chase, she was twenty-two when she signed for the show. She had first made a name for herself on skates – at the age of three when she was offered a job with Sonja Henie's troupe.

She was a fan of Fred's long before working on *Silk Stockings*. She had seen *Top Hat* and several of the other Astaire–Rogers films two or three times. When they first met, she was working on another lot nearby. Fred found his way to the set and watched her as she danced. 'It made me shake all over,' she recalled.

Fred paid her the usual compliments and drove her wild with his search for what might have seemed unreachable perfection. He would cuss, shout and make her run out of the room crying, but when she came back after two hours alone soothing her wounded pride, he would pretend that she had never been away.

He was not, she points out, a Santa Claus with frosting. The show was called *An Evening With Fred Astaire* – but like any other Fred Astaire production, the evening was really the result of several months of hard work.

David Rose, one of the most talented of Hollywood's music makers, conducted the orchestra and provided musical arrangements of numbers that ranged from 'Change Partners' and 'Baubles, Bangles and Beads' to 'A Foggy Day' and 'Top Hat, White Tie and Tails'.

He was amazed at the detail that went into preparing the dance routines. As he recalls: 'I walked into a rehearsal and there was dead silence for five minutes, with Fred and Hermes Pan just staring at each other. Then Hermes said to Fred that he had the answer to their problem. He should step off on the left foot instead of the right. They had been debating for fifteen minutes which foot to step out on. Every step he took just had to be accounted for.'

It was easy to see that the show lightly called a Fred Astaire 'Special' was special in many ways – and not just simply because it starred Fred Astaire. Previously, no one had even considered having more than a quintet or perhaps a sextet for a TV show. Astaire brought in David Rose to head a forty-piece orchestra.

As always it wasn't easy for anyone to get to know him. While Barrie Chase resorted to tears, Rose and Bud Yorkin the producer wondered why Fred kept himself so aloof. He didn't mix very much with the others on the set, simply concerned himself with getting out a perfect program. Not that it lessened their respect for him. As

Rose says: 'I was no different from anyone else in Hollywood. It was an honour to be with him.' He was not demanding at all. He just watched and said: 'Here, you know what to do.' The orchestra knew just what beats they would have to mark so that Fred could come on with the sort of precision he demanded.

The show was full of innovations. Fred did the unheard of thing and sang a medley of ten songs. The big risk, and the thing that worried Fred most, was that it was all live. The company had a once-only try at getting it right. As it turned out, they got it very right indeed. The show won nine Emmy awards.

The Emmy that Fred himself won for the best actor of 1958 – the show was aired on 17 October 1958 and repeated on 26 January 1959 – caused a row in the industry. Some critics said that it should have gone to a dramatic actor, not a dancer. When he heard that, Fred said he would give the Emmy back – but was persuaded to keep it.

Certainly, Fred's Special had set new standards. The original production had a rating of 18.9 – phenomenally high. The repeat registered a rating of 26.2. It was an encouraging sign that tapings of programmes, of which this was one of the very first, would be the big thing for the future.

The *New York Times* said: 'Mr Astaire's show enjoyed such individual distinction that it is probably not wise to draw too many conclusions from its success. In any case, the experience with Mr Astaire's show does invite interesting speculation.'

There was also some very interesting speculation about his relationship with Barrie Chase. Fred was constantly worried – among other things to be worried about – concerning suggestions that there was something immoral in his partnering a girl who was not only so attractive, but also so young. When critics commented that the pair represented a combination of June and December, he would light-heartedly ask: 'Couldn't they have said, June and October?'

However, for a time after the Special had been aired, they would go out for quiet dinners together.

Occasionally, he could be brought out to comment on the 'affair'. 'Barrie is a sweet girl of twenty-three,' he said. 'But I'm sure she's not interested in me. She is talented and we have much in common.'

People were still talking about their TV show together – and the effect it was likely to have on the industry. The taping of the show and its second performance had 'swept all before it', network executives reported excitedly – and asked for an immediate guarantee that there would be another Astaire–Chase outing on the box.

Fred was as enthusiastic about the idea as anyone else, but he had also been tickled by another proposition: Stanley Kramer wanted Fred to make a film for United Artists. It would be in black and white and his wouldn't even be the top name above the title. But it was too exciting a prospect to resist—he wouldn't have to dance a step or sing a note in it.

In the early 1960s, Fred turned more and more to television, gaining a regular spot as the host of Alcoa Theater.

In 1960, Fred and Barrie did another special, "Astaire Time". The show won two Emmys and was America's entry in the Golden Rose of Montreux competition.

In 1959, Fred Astaire produced his autobiography *Steps In Time*, with every word written by himself – because, he said, a ghost writer couldn't express his thoughts the way he felt them. The book would be, he believed, a chance to put those thoughts on record. Certainly, he had no intention of making a fortune out of what was never intended as a literary exercise.

One of the thoughts he expressed in that book was that he did not like challenges. Yet *On the Beach* was undoubtedly going to be the biggest challenge of his career. In this Stanley Kramer film, Fred played a British scientist involved in the last human journey following a nuclear holocaust. The year was supposed to be 1964, immediately after the entire northern part of the world had been devastated by the Bomb and just before the nuclear fallout was making its deadly way southwards. Gregory Peck was the commander of an American submarine working out in Australia, Anthony Perkins his junior officer and Ava Gardner the loose woman with whom Peck gets involved. Together, they and the scientist decide to make a journey back to the States in order to see what Armageddon had left behind. By the time they return to Australia that continent is as dead as everywhere else.

There seems nothing for any of them to do but patiently await death – so all four decide that if they are to die, they will do it in their own way. Perkins takes his wife aside and with her swallows a suicide pill; Peck takes the submarine back to America; Ava waits for a lonely end in Australia while the scientist extinguishes himself sitting in his racing car as the exhaust fumes sweep around him in the locked garage.

Fred said it took him thirty seconds to make up his mind to play the part of Julian Osborne, the scientist. Kramer had regarded Astaire's decision as proof enough that he did take up challenges.

'I've thought about doing straight roles,' Fred said at the time, 'but always hesitated and finally gave up the idea on the grounds that the public (or that part of the public who wants to see me at all) might not accept an Astaire who neither sang nor danced. I figured that if a director of his standing thought I could do it, that was security enough for me.'

He admitted he had had doubts over being able to do justice to the role – but was satisfied that Kramer didn't throw him out before the film was finished.

He said he had decided now, finally, not to do any more dancing pictures. The sceptic could have remarked that he had said that more than once before. But this time it did seem that he had finally made up his mind and with no reason to bluff, really meant it. 'I've done them all, you see. Over thirty pictures – and that just about exhausts the possibilities. I was determined not to become a dancing freak at sixty.'

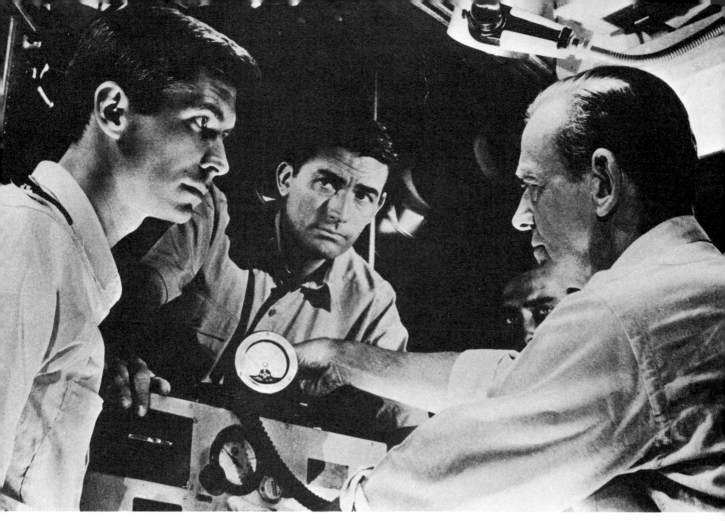

On the Beach *also starred Tony Perkins and Gregory Peck.*

It had certainly been something he had frequently thought about. A non-musical role became more a practical possibility, he felt, after the success of *Imp On A Cobweb Leash*.

Fred arrived back in the States to find that he was as much in demand as ever. Would he make another TV spectacular? Finally, he agreed that he would – but first he was going to do another straight role on television and would sport a beard for the occasion. This was *Man On A Bicycle* and was as enthusiastically received as the earlier play had been.

He followed it on 4 November 1959 with the second Special and again it was with Barrie Chase. 'Another Evening with Fred Astaire' had them doing a series of numbers that were as much tailored for their needs as the old repertoires had been for Fred and Ginger.

The past was still not something he wanted to talk about. 'Reminiscing is for the birds,' he declared more than once. 'Only the future counts.' And that was why he constantly turned down offers for *Steps In Time* as a possible film subject. 'I'm alive, not dead. Why go into the past? However much they offer me – and the offers come in all the time – I shall not sell.'

In On the Beach, *Nevil Shute's terrifying story of atomic war, Fred made his dramatic film debut as a nuclear physicist with a passion for fast automobiles. Here he is shown with co-stars Gregory Peck and Ava Gardner.*

For many, it was annoying that he wasn't being seen doing enough dancing. But in September 1960, he made his second spectacular with Barrie Chase in ten months, again with the same sponsor, Chrysler, and again with David Rose leading the music. The show, called now *Astaire Time*, won two Emmys. But Fred told Rose he wasn't sure he wanted to do any more. They were too time-consuming. Other stars who felt that Fred had given them the green light to go into the giant new medium themselves spent perhaps a week, occasionally just a day, planning their routines. Fred took three months at least and plenty of off-set work, too.

Fred's awards were not restricted to his television Emmys. In 1960, he received one of the three annual *Dance* Magazine prizes at a reception at the plush New York Athletic Club. The presentation was made by his first dancing partner – Adele.

A behind-the-scenes shot of Fred and Debbie Reynolds, taken during the filming of The Pleasure of his Company.

In May 1961, Fred starred with Debbie Reynolds in another straight role. This was *The Pleasure Of His Company*, based on a Broadway success. It was about a man meeting his former wife, Lilli Palmer, and his so-grown-up daughter, Debbie Reynolds, with whom he does dance, but only as any other straight actor might have danced if the action called for a ballroom scene.

The course of *The Pleasure Of His Company* did not run entirely smooth. The $3 million production had to grind to a halt when it was only half completed because a Screen Actors Guild strike closed all production. It was impossible to finish the work before Debbie Reynolds and Lilli Palmer were due to start new contractual engagements. So it was put into cold storage for six months.

Producer William Perlberg told Fred: 'You're 61, so please take it easy for the next six months. If you drop dead, we're finished.'

He survived and the film went back into production.

If, as Fred had said, he didn't like the 'chewing' over his age he could still joke about it. 'I know I've been in the business a long time,' he said on his sixty-second birthday. 'I used to be expected to kiss the leading lady on the lips. Now all I have to do is buss her on the forehead!'

In 1962, Fred had roles in five television straight plays, all of which fitted into the general heading of Fred Astaire's Premiere Theatre. Actually Fred was on the screen almost every week for two years, hosting the series in much the same way as Dick Powell and Alfred Hitchcock had done, but the five plays, *Mister Easy, Moment of Decision, Guest In The House, Mister Lucifer* and *Blues for a Hanging*, were the only ones in which he acted, too. It was yet another facet of the varied Astaire career. And like the other experiences in show business, he seemed to enjoy it all immensely.

His success secret – and it *was* a successful endeavour – was to realise that an audience could turn the switch at any moment. So he knew his task was to keep the people gripped. 'My theory is that if an audience stays ten minutes, it will stay to the end.'

His experience as a dancer was also an advantage. 'You move better.

You seem relaxed and that, I think, makes the audience feel more relaxed and more inclined to stick with you. At the same time, a dancer learns to hold an audience's attention by the way he moves. This gives the audience a sense of expectancy of growing excitement.'

That was much the same feeling film director Richard Quine had when he ensnared Fred to star in the film he was making for Columbia, *The Notorious Landlady*. Like *The Pleasure of His Company* and most other Astaire films the story line really wasn't important, the important thing was seeing Fred at work again. This time, it was about an American diplomat in London, and the intrigues revolving around his subordinate Jack Lemmon and his 'notorious' lady friend Kim Novak.

Quine wisely took advantage of what some other directors had chosen to ignore – the very thing that had people on the set gaping when Fred made his big musicals of the fifties. His walk. Fred didn't dance in the film, but his walk looked, as usual, as though it had been choreographed. And to exploit that walk, Quine made him march down a very long carpet, so that every movement could be seen by the audience.

He also supplied Fred with a pool table so that he could indulge his passion. It was not entirely a selfless thing to do. There was as much pleasure in watching him play pool as seeing him walk.

For two years, Fred Astaire's contact with the public was limited to the few people who managed to spot him in the streets of Beverly Hills, possibly doing a bit of shopping or perhaps driving one of the two Rolls Royces he now owned.

If people did come close enough to Fred to pin him down, it seemed they mostly wanted to know his opinion of the current dance and music crazes. What, for instance, did he think of the twist? 'I think it's great,' he said, 'a combination of the shimmy and the snake-hips. I stopped doing it fifteen years ago.'

In 1964, he was closely associated with another dance called the Watusi. It was featured in a play with music in which Fred danced yet again with Barrie Chase – who, had she been with him on the large screen, would by now have more than earned the title of the Second Ginger Rogers. Had she wanted it, that is. Chances are, she was more than happy being Barrie Chase.

Think Pretty was – as the *New York Times* put it – 'a hopelessly intricate and pedestrian story about the recording business. . . .' The paper's critic, Jack Gould, was kinder about Fred: 'For a few tanta- lising moments of seeing Fred Astaire dance once again, the viewers of last night's presentation of *Think Pretty* had to wait a long hour of ridiculous situation comedy.'

The moments of pleasure, insisted the writer, were all too rare.

'The prospect of seeing the couple in light and lilting movement turned out to be nothing but a come-on for routine silliness from Hollywood. The brief glimpses of Mr Astaire's rhythmic responses to melodies only compounded the feeling of being cheated. The pro-

In The Notorious Landlady, *Fred plays an American diplomat in London whose subordinate (Jack Lemmon) becomes involved with a young woman suspected of murder (Kim Novak).*

Fred and yet another of a long line of beautiful leading ladies, Kim Novak.

gramme's gag writers should have watched his feet for a lesson in the art of communication.'

Yet Fred was still 'the ageless dancer'.

In 1965, Fred surprised everyone by taking a subsidiary role in four episodes of the TV soap opera, 'Dr Kildare'. It was one of the better series, one that was exported, but a soap opera just the same. He followed it in January, March and April 1966 by hosting three variety shows in the Hollywood Palace series. Fred's television career seemed to be confusing Mrs Ann Astaire, who still lived with Fred and who in her late eighties was mostly very much aware of her surroundings. But every time she saw a commercial, she would call over to Fred: 'What are those people doing in your show?'

She liked doing things for herself. If she went out shopping, Fred would have to send his chauffeur out to bring her back.

In 1965, Fred did four episodes of Dr. Kildare, *with Richard Chamberlain.*

Meanwhile, Fred was rapidly losing enthusiasm for his excursion into the world of commerce, the Fred Astaire Dance Studios. He disposed of his interest although the chain still retained his name. Afterwards, the organisation came into difficulties with the Federal Trade Commissioner – who charged that the company 'operated in a misleading and coercive manner'. He ordered it to change its ways.

But if the Astaire Dance Studios were no longer his affair, the Fred Astaire career was – and he reacted to what he considered unwarranted criticism in the tried and true manner: not by sitting down and forgetting it, but by writing back to the critic.

A small magazine called *Films In Review* upset Fred and he pulled no punches in saying so.

He didn't like what he considered to be a snide comment on Fred's hair. The writer commented that Fred wore a 'dyed wig'. Said Astaire: 'I wore just exactly what I have always worn in all my recent TV specials and pictures.'

If people were talking about Fred's appearance – and the short, grey wig that he wore *was* both modern and stylish – it was nothing, compared with the shock experience of seeing the results of his first film in six years, *Finian's Rainbow*. It is now fairly obvious that this was to be his very last musical, the last picture in which Fred Astaire danced solo. But it was a very different Fred Astaire, stepping out very different dances.

It wasn't simply that he didn't wear a top hat, white tie and tails – as we have seen, he had grown fairly tired of that outfit. But the elegant, suave Fred Astaire was actually seen with at least two days' growth of beard, threadbare cuffs on his torn jacket and a naughty glint in his eyes. Nor was he doing a new version of the 'Couple of Swells' tramps number. This was all for real; all very much part of the story. He was a caricature of an Irish immigrant who had stolen a crock of gold from a leprechaun. Since America's wealth appeared to be buried at Fort Knox, here was his big opportunity to plant the stolen wealth nearby and wait to see if it would grow as he believed Fort Knox had grown.

A visit from Ava on the set of Finian's Rainbow.

Finian's Rainbow *is the story of a simple Irish immigrant who journeys to Fort Knox with a leprechaun's gold. It was directed by Francis Ford Coppola, who later directed* The Godfather, *and co-starred Petula Clark, the popular British singing star.*

165

He pranced and danced like a ten-year-old but he was, in fact, beginning to look his age. Even if that were deliberate, the effect was fairly shattering. *Finian's Rainbow* was a twenty-year-old story which had first seen the light of day on Broadway in 1947. It was then a sensation in the States, a flop in London. The best part of the film was undoubtedly Fred, both from the audience's point of view and from those of his co-stars, Tommy Steele as the leprechaun, and Petula Clark who played his daughter. It was a fascinating combination, Astaire and Clark. None of Fred's magic as a potential dancing partner had faded when Petula turned up on the set, petrified for her first try-out steps with Astaire.

There was more to their partnership than mere dancing, however. They also sang together, after the first recording had been completed and the tape played back, Fred jumped in the air and shouted: 'I sang with her! I sang with her!' It turned out that he had been as worried about matching up with her singing talents, the views of Cole Porter, Irving Berlin and the Gershwins notwithstanding, as she had been about dancing with him.

To Tommy Steele, too, it was a moment to treasure. Like everybody working on Astaire pictures before him, the young Cockney who had started his playing in a coffee-bar skiffle group was most impressed by the man's constant search for perfection – as detailed and intensive a search as for any crock of gold. Fred would work at the task from nine in the morning until six in the evening and carry on at weekends, too.

The critical comments at the time were mixed. Most of the adverse criticism came from Britain. The London *Evening Standard* commented: 'Now we know. There's schmaltz at the end of the rainbow.' The *Evening News* said: 'There's just a drop too much of the Oirish' and the *Daily Telegraph* headed their review: 'Blarney is to blame.'

Fred made it absolutely clear that *Finian's Rainbow* was definitely his last dancing picture. And now that he was past sixty-eight years-old, no one bothered to argue.

If people did think that perhaps the image of Fred in *Finian's Rainbow* confirmed that he was a seedy old man, something had to be done to alter the situation – and quickly. So Fred and Barrie Chase did another TV spectacular together. This was a much more up-to-date Astaire than even the other Specials had shown him to be. He appeared with such established figures of the late sixties musical scene as Simon and Garfunkel and Sergio Mendes.

The *New York Times* loved it: 'The tireless and ageless Fred Astaire bridged the generation gap last night in a precise display of footwork attuned to both popular old favourites and examples of such varied beats as come from the Young-Holt Trio, the Gordian Knot and the delicate compositions of Simon and Garfunkel.'

He certainly could dance with Barrie Chase and make people forget the years that were otherwise very much on their minds. The age difference seemed to gain very much more importance when they were seen together off the dance floor. And they *were* frequently seen together. Despite Fred's age, there were people who still tried to make an affair out of his friendship with Barrie Chase. Would they marry? The embarrassing questions continued and the only answers anyone got were from their close friends who said that they didn't think it likely – since Fred still felt his principal duty was to look after Ava.

In 1968, Ava married Carl Bostleman, Junior, an interior decorator who was a member of a Boston society family. The ceremony conducted by an Episcopalean minister was at Fred's house. The Astaire family – particularly Aunt Delly – were not very enamoured of the match, but Ava appeared to be greatly in love and Fred gave her away in marriage. Now all three Astaire children were married. Would that give Fred the opportunity to marry Barrie? The speculation grew – and amounted to nothing.

The trouble seemed to be that the more Fred Astaire did in films or television, the more people wanted to know about him. To be seen with a pretty young girl was virtually inviting a lynching by self-appointed moralists. They did nothing more than cause embarrassment. One can only imagine how Fred felt when 'an intimate little dinner party' which he attended after a Cole Porter festival at New York's Lincoln Centre turned out to be copy for the *Daily News* gossip writer Suzy. 'After swimming around in champagne for about an hour,' she wrote, 'the coruscant collection repaired to the first-floor dining room for a smart little supper, Adele Astaire . . . was all golden and glistening as she toyed with her salmon mousse.'

That could be one reason why Fred didn't like parties in the 1960s any more than he had thirty years before. He did, however, have that work bug again.

In the summer of 1968, Fred got all dressed up in cut-away coat, wing collar, cravat and a shiny black top hat – and was thrown out of Buckingham Palace. To those who were upset at the idea of a stubble-chinned Astaire the year before, the shame of seeing their idol turned away from the palace – where they thought he should feel so much at home – was beyond imagination.

The scene was for a film called *Midas Run*. But the thumbs-down actually happened to him. The picture in which Fred had third billing after Anne Heywood and Richard Crenna had a very slight story about a British civil servant who engineers the theft of gold bullion from Italy. It is all supposed to be a demonstration of the man's disgust at constantly being thwarted in his hopes of getting a knighthood.

When the plot succeeds beyond his wildest dreams, he finally makes the trip to the Palace to be dubbed by the Queen. He was supposed to stand by the gates, smile to the crowds whom everyone knew would be waiting there, and then march smartly across the courtyard.

It was at that moment that a policeman put up his hand and said that not even Fred Astaire could expect to get any further. The trouble was that the producer had not applied for a permit from the Lord Chamberlain's office before setting up the scene.

He had another worry, too. Everywhere he went, people asked 'Where's Ginger?' And it was nearly twenty years since his last picture with her and thirty years since the end of the series for RKO.

In London, he was annoyed when someone suggested he might make a comeback with Adele in *Lady Be Good*. As he said at the time: 'Have you ever heard anything so stupid? It's ludicrous. Do you know, I can barely remember the thing – beyond the fact that Adele and I enjoyed doing it.'

Midas Run was the nearest an Astaire film ever got to receiving an 'X' rating – since Miss Heywood was seen bare-breasted in a couple of sequences. They were filmed after he had finished work on the picture but they upset some of his most devoted fans. People wrote asking how he could possibly be associated with that sort of thing. Fred took the view that since he wasn't in the scenes himself, it didn't matter a damn to him.

Ava toyed with the idea of following Fred into the theatre in some capacity, but her domestic responsibilities took over instead. She introduced her father to some of her friends. Among them was Robert Wagner, the perennially young film actor who in an earlier age would have been listed in the casting directories as a juvenile, whom Fred had in fact known since he was nine years of age. Wagner was at the time starring in a series called 'It Takes A Thief'.

He said he would love Fred to play his father in an episode of the story being made at the end of 1969. The one episode became four — four very successful miniature movies which were repeated the following season. To Wagner it was a career milestone—particularly since Fred taught him how to make up as a clown. To Fred, it was yet another opportunity to demonstrate his versatility.

As for the future, he sat back now and contemplated: 'There's nothing I want to do that I haven't done. I don't give a damn if I never do another picture or another show. After all, you don't go on doing the same thing forever. If someone asks me to do something worth doing and I want to do it, then I will. But it will have to be awfully enticing to me.'

Yet come the enticements did.

168

No one expected much of Fred Astaire in the 1970s. His appearance was distinctly craggy and if you didn't watch the way he moved across the room – like one of his beloved racehorses ambling through the paddock – you might have been tempted to suggest that Fred's days as a great star were finally over.

He was in good health, but he knew it wouldn't be clever to try to tax his heart by doing the routines that had set him apart from every other hoofer in show business. If he *had* dwelt on the past, he might have decided that retirement was what he now wanted.

But he had other ideas. When Dick Cavett invited Fred to be the sole guest on his television show in November 1970, he took over the evening as though he were a young sprite proving to Broadway he was as good as his reviews said he was. He sat on a chair, talked to Cavett and did a dance or two.

A month later, he took on an appearance not totally different from the one he adopted in *Finian's Rainbow*, this time playing the sheriff to a bunch of equally superannuated Western characters in *The Over The Hill Gang Rides Again* for ABC Television.

Within four weeks of that, the Astaire voice was heard on another ABC show. This was yet another career first for him. His voice, together with those of Mickey Rooney, Keenan Wynn and Paul Frees, was superimposed in an animated TV film called *Santa Claus Is Coming To Town*.

His children were still vitally important to him and if none of them had chosen to follow in his footsteps, that was all right, too. Pete was a sheriff in Santa Barbara, Fred Junior had become a rather shy farmer and Ava had divorced Bostleman and married a tall artist called Richard McKenzie who bears a striking resemblance to Leonard Bernstein – and whom the family adored. The day that Ava and Richard were married, Fred was a judge at the annual Emmy award ceremony, so he could spend less than an hour with the couple. He found time, however, to pose for just one wedding group picture and kidded McKenzie: 'Look after my little girl and see that she looks after you.'

As far as he was concerned, he didn't look for souvenirs of his career and saw no reason why anyone else should either. But when one of the networks put on a late, late Astaire-Rogers film, it had the biggest mail bag for years in response. The insomniac audiences simply begged for more. Other networks followed suit and a big Astaire–Rogers revival was under way.

Fred tried not to see his films on television. But on one occasion, he did have the set switched on when an Astaire film was playing. 'And I had to stay to the end to see what happened.' He admitted at the time: 'There was a pretty good routine in it. I was pleased with that. In fact, it looked so darn good, I wondered how I ever did it. It would be awful if those routines looked crummy now. It would kinda make your life look pretty foolish, pretty empty.'

Continuing his dapper image, Fred plays a James Bond–type British Secret Service officer who masterminds a hi-jacking of gold ingots in The Midas Run. *Anne Heywood is his beautiful co-star.*

Anything that made him look old-fashioned was guilty of the biggest sin of all, so he agreed that he had to show the public what he was still capable of. In October 1971, he made a second solo appearance on the Dick Cavett Show and for ninety minutes left no one watching in any doubt that he was still an entertainer to study. He followed that three months later by hosting a tribute to his friend George Gershwin in a show called ''S Wonderful, 'S Marvellous, 'S Gershwin.' He was joined in this, among others, by Jack Lemmon, Ethel Merman and Peter Nero.

Ava agrees that he might not have carried on working had her mother still been alive, but even in the 1970s it still represented that irresistible enticement.

He did another TV show called 'Make Mine Red White and Blue' in September 1972 – when he was already seventy-three. In the following January, he had a cameo walk-through part in the John Lennon and Yoko Ono film *Imagine*, which just proved that he wasn't frightened off by the newer crowd.

Fred Astaire was now as magic a name and as recognizable as ever. When the new Uris Theatre was opened on Broadway, more eyes were focused on Fred and his first dancing partner Adele than any-one else. Fred tried not to let too many photographers come near them, but Adele loved every minute of it—and answered the clicking camera-men by taking her own pictures of Fred and every other celebrity around and about.

At home in Beverly Hills, their mother, fast approaching her century, was very much still in charge of looking after her 'Sonny'. At the age of ninety-five, she fell off a chair on which she had been standing to examine some curtains and broke a hip – but she recovered and agreed to use a wheel chair in future.

He kept in touch with a lot of his old friends – occasionally, for instance, playing golf with Bing Crosby or talking on the telephone with Irving Berlin.

When Fred met Gene Kelly they would just occasionally talk dancing. 'The bane of our mutual existence,' said Kelly, 'is that the critics tend to compare us. We had two different styles. If I put on a white tie and tails I look like a truck driver going out.'

Every now and again, Fred would still have dinner with his old friends, Hermes Pan and Ann Miller.

But the cinema still remains an important part of his life and he considers it his duty to see all the films being shown in what used to be the movie capital and when it comes to the annual Oscar selections, Fred goes to most of the films so that he can cast his vote knowledgably as a member of the Academy.

Early in 1973, Fred had found himself a new task – be it ever so reluctantly. The Film Society of the Lincoln Centre in New York

In 1971, Fred did two 90-minute solos with ABC's Dick Cavett.

With co-host Gene Kelly in MGM's That's Entertainment, Part 2.

171

Three of the greatest entertainers of all time—Frank Sinatra, Gene Kelly, and Fred, at Kelly's Friar's Club roast in 1975.

announced they would hold a gala in his honour. It would be a black-tie occasion, one that they hoped would raise something like $85,000 towards the society's funds.

Fred had to be talked into it – it all seemed rather like exposing himself in public and he was reluctant to do that. But he finally agreed and, in particular, consented to select thirty-five clips from his films – no mean task, considering there were something like two hundred numbers in thirty-one pictures to choose from.

'I see the list and wonder how the devil I did so much,' he said after the bulk of the task was completed. But, in case anyone got the wrong idea, he was quick to add: 'We laugh at those old pictures Ginger and I. We're good friends. But I don't want to go on talking about them the rest of my life. I live in the present.'

When the big evening arrived, the entire Philharmonic Hall was packed to overflowing. Finally, after the clips had been shown, Fred stood up in his box, dressed, as the Christian Science *Monitor* reported 'in a black tie and wide smile'. Adele was standing next to him to provide moral support and nearby were an assortment of her successors as leading ladies – Cyd Charisse, Joan Fontaine, Arlene Dahl and, of course, Ginger Rogers. Ginger, stunning in her platinum blonde coiffure, took a bow when Fred referred to her.

'I've got to go easy,' he said in his little speech, fighting to get the words out. 'There's so much emotion here – this is the most exciting thing that's happened to me. It's hard to describe the feelings of affection and appreciation.'

The organisers wondered whether an audience's attention could be sustained for nearly two hours of just seeing clips of old films; beginning with Clark Gable saying to him in *Dancing Lady*: 'Oh, Freddy, will you run through that number now?'

Every clip received an ovation from the 1200 people who had paid between $10 and $100 a ticket. Some 'honorary benefactors' paid $1,000 and even the press were expected to pay to get in – and did so willingly.

Later, a reception was held to Count Basie's music at the nearby New York State Theatre, where dozens of fans lined up to shake Fred's hand, to kiss him or just to collect an autograph. About half an hour after shyly walking in, Fred and Adele retired with the guests cheering them on their way. Some of them were dancing, doubtless imagining that for a moment, they, too, were Fred Astaire and Ginger Rogers.

So was this the end of Astaire in show business? Had all the cheers meant that Fred had had his swansong – and swandance? If anyone thought so, they were soon put right.

Early in 1974, Fred and Adele were seen in public again – and this time they did do a step or two. The successors to MGM had put together a massive collection of clips from the time when the letters stood for 'Makers of Good Musicals' and called it *That's Entertainment*.

In his recent film, The Towering Inferno *(1975), Fred returns to the dance floor in a cameo role with partner Jennifer Jones.*

Still the classic American dance team—Astaire and Rogers.

Fred and Adele Astaire at the Fred Astaire Festival at New York's Lincoln Center for the Performing Arts in 1973.

Fred was one of the 'hosts', linking the various segments of film and began with a demonstration of how shabby the train that had been used in *The Band Wagon* had become. What it really demonstrated was how perfect the musical and Astaire had been.

A year later, Fred and Gene Kelly did a similar job with a sequel, *That's Entertainment Part Two*. In between, however, Astaire was nominated for an Oscar, for the best supporting actor of the year. He didn't win the Academy Award, but the picture in which he had been featured was to be remembered principally for the Astaire role – a con man in *Towering Inferno*.

He didn't have stubble on his face this time, but there was no pretence at making him anything but a con man who was ageing. And when he danced – as he did, even if only in a ballroom scene with dozens of other people – it for once didn't matter that his partner, Jennifer Jones, looked rather taller than he did.

Fred and Ginger came together again for a brief moment in February 1975, a moment that recalled their past glories. Fred was made a member of the Entertainment Hall of Fame in Hollywood – an honour reserved for 'Twentieth century creators and performers for what they did that will last.'

Arriving in Nice, France, for the 1975 Film Festival. Besides Fred, the photo includes Marge Champion,
Gene Kelly, Cary Grant, Kathryn Grayson, Cyd Charisse, and Johnny Weismuller.

LET'S FACE THE MUSIC AND DANCE

Fred Astaire will never dance again in a film and when he next makes a picture he will be unlikely to carry the cane that came to symbolise the debonair Mr Twinkletoes. If he did, people might think he was using it for support.

At seventy-seven Fred needed neither physical nor moral support. He had established not merely a branch of show business that was all his own, but had found an acceptance that bordered on idolatry, as well as a place in the history books. The man who had been dubbed the Entertainer of the Century was something more than that; he was and is a phenomenon of his time.

Ask him why he has succeeded and he will probably put it all into his idea of historical perspective: 'If I were a young dancer trying out for a part in the movies today,' he said in 1974, 'I'd never make it. My one natural talent is dancing and that wouldn't get me much of a part in a modern screen musical. I'd probably end up in the chorus of *Hair* or *Godspell* or something. A lead dancer nowadays needs to be a combination of choreographer, actor and singer.' Which, of course, is exactly what Fred Astaire always has been – although he insists: 'I was never a fan of my own voice and I never really got a chance to act.'

He began in vaudeville, starred on Broadway and made a new career out of television. But it was in the movies that Astaire came into his own. And it is to the movies that he has always looked closest – first to study the market, more recently with something of a paternal air. He says the X-rated film has cheapened Hollywood and he cannot understand why exhibitors are allowed to show pictures that a few years ago would have had you arrested if you tried to screen them in your own front room. But now he says he detects an improvement on the way. 'All the signs make me extremely optimistic.' He thinks it good that producers go out of the studio to make their films, for instance.

Fred remains a very religious man. It was his religious faith which he insists sustained him during Phyllis's illness. Now, he can be seen most weeks at a small Beverly Hills church, taking part in the worship as an ordinary member of the congregation.

He doesn't like the harping on age – although even he admits he has been old for a long time. The past still does not interest him. 'I see the occasional movie. I like dramatics and that's it. That's my life story.'

Because he does not think of the past, he enjoys the present, although nothing will ever be the same as when he had Phyllis at his side, and every time he has a big success, his one wish is that she were with him to share it.

Rouben Mamoulian who had directed him in *Silk Stockings* said about him: 'He's a supreme artist. But he is constantly filled with doubts and self anger about his work – and that's what makes him good. He's a perfectionist who is never sure he is attaining perfection.'

One of his friends put it almost as seriously: 'He will probably be playing Hamlet at a hundred and ten.' It remains one of the few things he has not done – so far.

Just a couple of song and dance men.

177

But then he has always known his limitations – or claimed that he has. A few years ago someone predicted that he would still be dancing when he was ninety. 'The hell I will!' he said then. 'I guess the one thing that worries me is knowing when to stop. I don't give a hoot about clinging to a career. I don't want to become the oldest living dancer in captivity, a freak, a sideshow or antiquity.' So we can chalk that up to Fred Astaire, too – he knew when finally to put away those dancing shoes.

As for himself: 'I don't understand what people see in me. I don't look like a movie star and I don't act like a movie star. I'm just an old So and So from Omaha.'

And what about those people who talk about the 'art' of Fred Astaire? Those who belittle his originality and say that he was a second Nijinsky? To them he always has the same answer: 'I don't really know how the dance started and I don't give a damn where it's going. I don't think about art. All I know is that there were musical comedies with people dancing, so that's what I did. I just danced.'

Fred Astaire in 1975.

PHOTO CREDITS

The author and publishers wish to express their appreciation to the following for permission to use their photographs in this book:

Associated Press, p. 3, p. 104, p. 142, p. 174 left; The Bettmann Archive, Inc., p. 6 bottom right, p. 7 top, p. 7 bottom, p. 9, p. 14, p. 37 left, p. 48 top left, p. 53, p. 65, p. 70, p. 78, p. 82 bottom, p. 86, p. 96, p. 99 top, p. 99 bottom, p. 108, p. 109, p. 126, p. 127, p. 156 top; British Broadcasting Company, p. 58, p. 100 bottom, p. 105 bottom, p. 106, p. 110 bottom, p. 124, p. 141, p. 145 top, p. 149, p. 155, p. 161, p. 171 top; Brown Brothers, p. 5 left, p. 8, p. 12, p. 15, p. 16, p. 17, p. 24, p. 28, p. 31, p. 32, p. 34 right, p. 34 top left, p. 34 bottom left, p. 37 right, p. 41, p. 114 top, p. 115, p. 125, p. 128 top left, p. 129 right, p. 131 top, p. 134, p. 137 top, p. 153, p. 154, p. 156 bottom, p. 159; Culver Pictures, p. 2, p. 5 bottom right, p. 6 bottom left, p. 33, p. 35, p. 48 bottom left, p. 50, p. 74, p. 77 top, p. 77 bottom, p. 81, p. 94, p. 97, p. 100 top, p. 102, p. 119 bottom, p. 122, p. 128 center, p. 129 left, p. 130, p. 131 bottom, p. 140, p. 144, p. 145 bottom, p. 169; Michael Freedland, p. 60, p. 179; Globe Photos, p. 83, p. 150-151, p. 157, p. 162, p. 164, p. 165; National Film Archive, p. 4, p. 11, p. 19, p. 45, p. 48 right, p. 55, p. 57, p. 66, p. 72, p. 105 top, p. 112, p. 113, p. 114 bottom, p. 117, p. 136, p. 137 bottom, p. 163, p. 171 bottom, p. 176; Radio Times Hulton Film Library, p. 5 top right, p. 21, p. 22, p. 23, p. 40, p. 44; Springer/Bettmann Film Archive, p. 6 top, p. 18, p. 38, p. 42, p. 46-47, p. 49, p. 62-63, p. 68-69, p. 80, p. 82 top, p. 84, p. 87, p. 91, p. 93, p. 110, p. 111, p. 118, p. 119, p. 123, p. 128 top right, p. 128 bottom, p. 135, p. 160 top, p. 160 bottom; United Press International, p. 36, p. 64, p. 132, p. 148, p. 172, p. 173, p. 174 right, p. 175.